THE BRUISED REED AND SMOKING FLAX.

" They know the Almighty's love,
Who, when the whirlwinds rock the topmost grove,
Stand in the shade and hear the tumult,—
Curb'd by some power unseen, fast die away."

THE BRUISED REED

AND SMOKING FLAX

BY

RICHARD SIBBES, D.D.

WITH INTRODUCTORY ESSAY

BY

ALEXANDER BEITH, D.D.

EDINBURGH: MACLAREN & MACNIVEN.
LONDON: J. NISBET & CO.
STIRLING: J. MACFARLANE, *Drummond's Tract Depot.*
1878.

Printed by FRANK MURRAY, *11 Young Street, Edinburgh.*

CONTENTS.

Contents.

Contents.

INTRODUCTORY ESSAY.

———◆———

Biographical ;—Puritan Doctrine Calvinistic ;—The Gospel has ever been. the Same—A Message of Goodwill—Unites Warning and Instruction ;—Noah's Experience—Illustrations ;— Relief from the Great Burden, Sin, makes Smaller Burdens Light ;—Job.

Dr. Richard Sibbes, the author of the Treatise to which the following Notice is introductory, was one of the most celebrated of the Puritans of the seventeenth century. Though his life was not a protracted one, for he died in his fifty-eighth year, yet in his time he accomplished important work as an expounder of Divine truth, as an earnest advocate of sound doctrine, and an eloquent preacher of the glorious Gospel of the blessed God.

Dr. Sibbes was of humble parentage. His father was a wheelwright, in the town of Tostock, in Suffolk, where our author was born, A.D. 1597. No higher destiny for his son was thought of by the father than that he should follow his profession, and be his successor in the business which he had formed. The preliminary education deemed necessary to qualify him for this brought to light the natural genius inherent in the boy. He became eminent at school—the Free School of Bury St. Edmunds—so much so as to attract the attention of a dignitary of the Church. By the influence of this generous man, the position of an under-sizar of St. John's College, Cambridge, was acquired for young Sibbes. The presentation entitled him to a sort of public, pauper, College education. Of the Institution in question, there are, or there were, three grades — the *sizar,* the *under-sizar, and the poor scholar.* The medium class was that of Sibbes. The lowest class was that of Jeremy Taylor—his contemporary—who, in after life, became one of the most illustrious of the men of his day. To be a student at Cambridge in any grade was much a privilege. It opened the way to preferment; and, where talent existed and was drawn forth, to eminence and usefulness in life. Thus the intended wheelwright of Tostock was introduced to a line of progress by which he advanced to the great distinction in the world of literature and theology which he ultimately attained. In no long time, such was the estimate formed of his character, he was elected College preacher. Soon thereafter, by the grace of God, he became a savingly converted man. To this fact strong testimony is borne by those who were acquainted with the circumstances which marked the event, though he is himself silent on the subject. Other appointments followed that of College preacher, under circumstances which gave evidence of the high esteem in which he was held, not only by the cultivated classes in Cambridge, but also by the country population in the neighbourhood of the city. LAUD, however, had his eye—no friendly eye—set on the rising youthful evangelist. Jeremy Taylor had secured the Archbishop's favour and patronage. Sibbes had not. So, whilst the former was advanced by the semi-Popish pretender to Protestant orthodoxy, the latter was deprived—was driven from his Cambridge lectureship, as well as from other appointments.

In this emergency, the interference of an influential and, at the time well-known friend and patron of godly ministers—such as the good Lord of the kingdom has, in all times of trial in His Church, raised up—procured for our author the preachership of Gray's Inn, London, an appointment more important than that of which he had been deprived. Thus, that in which Laud had thought evil against him, God meant unto good: it fell out for "the furtherance of the gospel." This appointment he retained for life; whilst also, at a subsequent period, he was restored to his Cambridge office, and so held both charges.

As the officiating minister of Gray's Inn, Sibbes came to be associated with many persons of high rank, as well as of literary distinction. His was a time when great names, not a few, graced the social circles of the metropolis, names which have descended to our times, and which will be transmitted to coming generations. Deeply interesting it is to reflect that the advantage of such Gospel preaching—searching, faithful, earnest—as that of Sibbes, was enjoyed by men like Lord Bacon, Cromwell, and Shakespeare. Even Milton may sometimes, in early youth, have listened to this popular Calvinistic Puritan, pouring forth, Sabbath after Sabbath, in such strains of heavenly thought as are exemplified in the treatise before us, the counsel of God for man's salvation. Whatever the case may be as to Milton, when one happens to read simultaneously in the writings of Lord Chancellor Bacon, and in the writings of Richard Sibbes, he cannot fail occasionally to imagine that the one has been borrowing from the other—which from which it may be difficult to decide—though the probability is felt to be that the philosopher is more debtor to the divine than the divine to the philosopher. It is not impossible that the fall of the latter from his political eminence—his banishment, until near the close of his life, into the shade of court disfavour and comparative obscurity, touching which we may believe the ex-Chancellor and his minister held not infrequent friendly converse—led to the production of the treatise to which the reader is in these pages introduced, and inspired the genius of the author, so manifest in all its parts. A "bruised reed" the great Chancellor did, with reference to his humiliating change of condition, denominate himself; and thus it may be no unwarrantable assumption that to Sibbes' sympathy with a broken-hearted man and to his pity for him we owe the sweet words of consolation and encouragement with which this treatise abounds. Not that such influence as we refer to explains all. Bacon may have been much on Sibbes' heart as he preached his discourses; but the case of all whom God teaches in the school of affliction, and whom in every age He so prepares for Himself—for His service now, and for glory hereafter—must have been much more so. Our author's own heavy trial, too, by his second and latest deprivation, shared in common with so many of his brethren, under the pressure of which some of them were compelled, for their personal safety, to flee their country, must have had its effect on his sensitive mind. Private influence, originating in the high value set on his ministrations and the earnest desire to retain these, availed to preserve him from the pressure of the necessity which compelled the painful course adopted by his friends. Sibbes consequently continued, until the close of his life, to discharge the duties of Preacher in Gray's Inn—tolerated, and no more than tolerated, by those who frowned upon him, but honoured by those who delighted in his ministry.

Sibbes was an advocate, in his time, of what men call Calvinism. He, no doubt, studied the writings of the great Reformer. In his time these must have been comparatively recent publications, making it possible that he was not greatly conversant with them. However that may be, we are quite warranted to believe that the source from which Calvin drew his stores of Divine knowledge was that from which Sibbes procured, in like manner, his treasures. Both were equally debtors to the same inspired Record, and to the same "unction from the Holy One," by which they were made to know all things. It is the fruit of a groundless fancy to ascribe to Calvin the origin of the doctrines to which his name has been attached. This is done by those who delight to impugn the doctrines, because they dislike them. It is easier, and safer for their reputation, to condemn Calvin than to condemn inspired Paul.

In the ages which preceded Calvin, as in the centuries which have followed his time, the doctrines in question, in every line of them, have been embraced and maintained by all true students of Holy Writ. Thousands who have never had opportunities to be taught Calvinistic doctrine, who have never read a sentence of his, but who, under conviction of sin, and alarms of conscience, earnestly searching for relief and comfort, have been led to the one fountain of the knowledge necessary to salvation, have thence been enlightened, and so learned the same truths. When they subsequently, as in some instances has happened, became acquainted with the dogmatic teachings of the great theological master, they have been filled with wonder to find that, by their own investigations, they had anticipated his teaching, as well as the teachings of all other human authorities, having been made wise from above.

Whatever may be said of the literary acquirements of our author, and the process through which he became so great a master in that department, we may safely conclude that the theological acquirements, which so eminently qualified him for the sacred work of the pulpit, were mainly derived direct from the Scriptures of truth, under the effectual saving application of the Spirit of truth.

The Gospel, as to its distinctive virtue, has always been the same. Therein we have the answer of the Father in heaven to the cry of the awakened soul—the soul enlightened through the knowledge of the truth, and brought face to face with the awfully solemn realities of its relations to Him, the Most High. Slumber, a death-like slumber as to those realities, is the normal condition of all of us. In the case of those who are ultimately saved, a time comes when the slumber is broken—broken it may be as by the crash of a thunder peal, or as by the loving touch

of a friendly hand—but broken it is, and compelled
to yield to convictions never known before. In
vain shall any man attempt satisfactorily to describe
the change of mind which ensues to those who have
not themselves experienced this change. We do not
refer to temporary agitations and disturbances, produced by short-lived convictions and alarms arising
from various causes, of which there are too many
examples. We refer to convictions which are produced by the life-giving influences of the quickening
Spirit; as different from the other as the action con-
nected with the returned consciousness of a half-
drowned man, in whom there is life, is different from
the action imparted to a dead carcase by the application of the power which issues from the galvanic
battery. The one is permanent, and ends in life; the
other is evanescent, done at the will of the operator,
and ends in the condition of death from which there
had really been no deliverance.

God's message comes to the soul. It is a message, first of warning, then of instruction. The veil
is lifted off the future, our own personal future;
the ruinous delusions of a worldly life are dis-
pelled; the responsibilities as to the world unseen
are disclosed; danger of " everlasting destruction from
the presence of the Lord, and from the glory of His
power," is so set before our eyes that we cannot
banish the sight. It is as when the manslayer who,
but a moment ago, lived in the happiness of con-
scious innocence, unexpectedly sees on his hands the
blood of his neighbour—sees that he has become
amenable to the behests of the avenging law which

requires that he who sheddeth man's blood, by man shall his blood be shed.   As that offender's peaceful security has vanished, as his quietude has disappeared, as the demand for instant flight presses itself on his consideration and produces the necessary immediate race for life, so it is in the case of the savingly awakened sinner.   He is "lost;" and he now knows it.   What is he to do? whither is he to look?   In what refuge, if in any, is he to find shelter?   The Gospel provides the answer.   Thence the answer comes, and thence only :—thence only, with effect, when the awakening is genuine ; when the Spirit of God, in pursuance of the gracious Divine purpose, has produced it ; and when the fruits in the inner man are such as His power alone can produce.   When *He* "kills," *He* must "make alive ;" when *He* "wounds," *He* must "heal ;" for there is none "that can deliver out of His hand." "*He* maketh sore and bindeth up ; *He* woundeth and *His* hands make whole."

To Noah, God sent His message, with a view to the patriarch's salvation.   "The end of all flesh," the Lord said, "has come before me ; for the earth is filled with violence through them ; and, behold, I will destroy them with the earth."   Noah was "moved"— awakened to such a sense of danger as he had never known.   More or less, he must previously have been affected by his painful associations with the world in which he lived—associations which he could not avoid, and from which he could not escape.   However he may have been "vexed" with these, never had he been "moved"—"moved with fear"—cast into a condition of awakened alarm, such as he now experienced.   The coming calamity which had been revealed was not to occur immediately. It was future—comparatively distant. Moreover, it was "unseen as yet:" no portent, no terrifying signals of approaching doom, no "sign" occurred to sadden the heart. But Noah's faith made the *future*, though thus qualified, an imminent *present;* and his soul panted for the instruction by which he might obtain relief and peace. God's message included that. He who knew the full import of the warning which had produced agitation in the mind of Noah, knew also what only could truthfully meet the emergency, and be a reliable ground of comfort. "*Make thee an Ark*" was the instruction: "Make thee an Ark !"—including, withal, stringent directions as to its structure, its dimensions, its character in all points.

By faith, we are distinctly informed, the change— the conversion—in the case of Noah was produced. By faith he accepted God's message in both its parts. By faith he was obedient to the heavenly call. By faith he became "heir of the righteousness which is by faith;" and so, by that which is "the substance of things hoped for, the evidence of things not seen," he, with others, whom the sacred Record enumerates, " obtained a good report."

Sinners, wherever the Gospel message comes, are warned of impending wrath—the wrath of God which is "revealed from heaven against all ungodliness and unrighteousness of men "—against sin, against all sin —sin whether in Jew or in Gentile, "for there is no difference :"—necessarily so revealed, that God's righteous government may be vindicated and upheld, that His Majesty may not be despised:—revealed in view, not only of present conditions, but in view, as well, of the conditions of His moral universe "in the ages to come."

To be savingly taught of the Spirit produces conviction. The soul fears; the soul is "moved" with fear; it trembles at God's Word. This is undoubtedly *due* to the truth. The case must be bad indeed with any man, who enjoys Gospel privileges, by whom this is not felt. Under conviction of the truth referring to God's law and its claims, the cry must become— "What shall I do?"—"What shall I do to be saved?"

The Gospel, as we have said, is provided for the emergency which has this issue. The message of warning never comes apart from the message of instruction. The instruction comes from Him who knows the case, who knows all that is included therein. "Behold the Lamb of God:" "Believe in the Lord Jesus Christ," is the authoritative instruction—instruction which makes known to the awakened, believing, soul how God's righteousness is now revealed—now revealed, not in the destruction of the sinner whom the law condemns, but in his salvation, on the ground of the glorious "propitiation":—revealed in the remission of sin, in the justification of the sinner's person —of the sinner accepting the truth, and casting himself on the faithfulness of God in Christ Jesus.

No evidence in proof of the truth referring to the coming deluge was given to Noah beyond the clear simple testimony of the Divine revelation. God had spoken it: that was all; and that was enough. Nothing in the heavens or on the earth came to corroborate the WORD. All nature, and nature in every form, was silent. No doubt men, scoffing, were found often to say, "Where is the promise of His coming?" It mattered not. The thing was true. God had spoken. Noah did not speculate, nor make enquiry beyond this. The Word of the Lord had come, and all with him was believing.

The whole action of his life, from this time forth, was produced by his *belief.* Such industry as he required to use to secure the means of subsistence for himself and his family, he, no doubt, employed. But the paramount object of his life had become that which the Word of the Lord demanded; on the authority of which, and under the convictions produced by which, he proceeded in all he did; becoming a preacher of the righteousness which is by faith, Christ speaking by him to the world; building the Ark, and, in doing so, condemning the world which either disregarded, derided, or resisted. His faith had this as its special fruit. As to his action with reference to the "meat which perisheth," being necessary, he must have given himself to it; but that action was subordinate to the other; was pursued only that he might meet the claims of the other, and so at length finish his course with joy.

Whilst Noah simply obeyed the Word which had been addressed to faith in him; whilst he had conscientious respect to the Divine method, in every line thereof, appointed for his salvation in view of the coming destruction, in nothing thinking his own thoughts, nor adopting the thoughts of others, as to this method —he must have had, at the same time, an intelligent sense of the suitableness, the competency, and the adequacy of God's plan.   He knew that the deliverance was to be a deliverance from a *flood*.   The method of his coming escape had respect to the form in which the great overthrow was to occur, of which he must have had some intelligent apprehension. What was required was not a method of escape from war, or from famine, or from pestilence.   Had it been either of these, the building of an ark would have been a vain conceit—foolishness.   He knew that by a flood, which should cover the face of the whole earth, judgment was to be inflicted.   His apprehension of the nature and full extent of this calamity may have been very inadequate.   It was enough that he was convinced that God knew all, and that the means of deliverance, being of Him, must be adequate, competent, and must prove sufficient.

We know not what may be included in the "wrath revealed against all ungodliness and unrighteousness" of ours.   "Who knoweth the power of His anger?" There may be involved an infinity of evil, which our minds are incapable even of conceiving.   The only standard by which the evil may be measured is the vicarious sufferings of the Son of God in His humanity, and as substituted in our stead—the humiliation; the agony of body and soul which he endured!   But who—angel or man—is capable of comprehending what that suffering included; that which is the only measure of the evil of sin?   And who will venture to say that that suffering was more than was meet?   Who will aver that less might have sufficed; that God was cruel, rigorous, or unjust to the Saviour? Who will presume to persuade himself that God will mete out to the sinner less than he sent upon the Substitute—to the sinner refusing, or neglecting, or contemning the great Sacrifice?

Who can tell what is required that there may be forgiveness of sin in the case of transgressors such as we ? Who can tell what is required that there may be satisfactory reason why the Most High, without injury to the glory of His character or the sacred rights of His Eternal Son, may accept the person and the services of the sinner; bestow on him the adoption of a son; the spirit of a son; the heirship and the inheritance of a son; and the full qualification for glory, with the crown of glory in the end? God Himself only can tell. As He only could instruct Noah to provide satisfactorily for the calamity that was "not seen as yet," but was sure as to its advent, so He only can tell what shall be sufficient to meet all the necessities of our case—the case of each of us—our necessities, in presence of temptations with which we are assailed; the inherent corruption which gives to temptations the power they so fatally exercise; the influence which, not only the Prince of this world, but the world itself, exerts; the terrors of disease and of death; the incomprehensibly solemn awards of the great judgment? God only knows what is before us, what awaits each of us ! God only, therefore, knows the provision required, the salvation which, if it be not ours, we are lost. His decision, therefore, in all this must be final and without appeal. No folly can equal the folly of, in such a matter, setting up our judgment as against, or in arrest of, His. No folly can equal the folly of men who wantonly attempt to minimise the evil of sin on the one hand, and the claims of law and justice on the other; comforting themselves with the worship of a God who is not the God of the Scripture; acting so, not on the principle of Noah when he believed God and built the ark, but on the principle of the spirits who are now in " prison," and who, in Noah's time, acted as in our time their successors act, when they yield themselves to persuasions that have no foundation but in the deceived heart which has turned them aside.

He is a faithful minister of Christ who proclaims these things.   Such a minister was Noah.   He is also an *accepted* minister who proclaims these things— accepted of those who have been awakened of God, who have been quickened, and who are crying out to be told of the way of life.   Nothing can give relief, can give peace that may be trusted, but the full and faithful exhibition of the glorious truth of Christ's substitution; of the great atonement; and of the all-prevailing intercession at the right hand of God.— A minister of such truth was Sibbes throughout all his course.

When the Gospel has been made effectual for our recovery in the matter of our great loss; effectual for bringing us home to our Father's house; effectual for making us partakers of the rich provision to be found there and there only, it is easy to see how the same Gospel must become the healing element in every lesser affliction which may befal us in our new condition. These afflictions are not few; neither are they uniform in character; nor do they all come from the same source. However all that may be, the Gospel proclaims the remedy for all, inasmuch as the Gospel ever sends the soul to Christ, the good Physician. When we go to Him, the afflictions are experienced to be light; for a moment; working out an eternal weight of glory. The reed which erewhile emitted, in the hand of him who played well on his instrument, its sweet sounds, may be "bruised;" its sweet sounds may never be heard again. Hope that they shall ever be may have all but perished. But He in whom we trust can meet the case. He will not "break," nor cast hopelessly aside the *bruised,* crushed thing. He will restore it; and yet again, His breath filling it, the melody of joy and health shall be heard therefrom, all the more that the instrument has been restored by the hand which at first made it. The flax may be reduced so that the evidence of life may be no more than the smoke which ascends from it in flickering waves. Can it revive? Can it be rekindled? Yes; the breath of the Spirit of Christ will come. He himself will come, not to quench, but to make it burn again, and to give forth the splendour of its cheerful light.

If our great sorrow be cured, all lesser sorrows will certainly be so. Let us betake ourselves to Him who is pledged to fulfil in His people "the good pleasure of His goodness." Our case may be peculiar, but never so bad but that He can reach and meet it. "Only believe," He says: Be not afraid; believe, and thou shalt see the glory of the Lord! "When thou passest through the waters I will be with thee; and through the rivers, they shall not overflow thee : when thou walkest through the fire thou shalt not be burned; neither shall the flame kindle on thee. For I am the Lord thy God, the holy One of Israel, thy Saviour."

"The heart knoweth his own bitterness." He who keeps the heart—to whom Israel are as the apple of the eye—knows it too. A calm, even a smiling, countenance may hide a heavy heart. A "stranger" does not discover it. He who will not break the bruised reed, nor quench the smoking flax, does. In Job's most prosperous days there was a weight on his heart. Who knew it? *He* did to whom Job's prayer, day and night, ascended in anxiety for his sons and daughters, lest they should forget God amidst their family happiness. Of his *care* he said, "I was not in safety, neither had I rest, neither was I quiet." Could worse be? Yes. "Yet trouble came :" he adds. "The thing which I greatly feared came." Was the bruised reed broken, then? Was the smoking flax quenched? No.

"Ye have heard of the patience (suffering) of Job, and have seen the end of the Lord; that the Lord is very pitiful, and of tender mercy."

A. B.

EDINBURGH, *May 1878.*

THE BRUISED REED AND SMOKING FLAX.

" A bruised reed shall he not break, and smoking flax shall he not quench, till he send forth judgment unto victory."—MATT. XII. 20.

CHAP. I.—*The Text opened and divided.   What the Reed is, and what the bruising.*

THE prophet Isaiah being lifted up, and carried with the wing of prophetical spirit, passeth over all the time between him and the appearing of Jesus Christ in the flesh, and seeth with the eye of prophecy, and with the eye of faith, Christ as present, and presenteth him, in the name of God, to the spiritual eye of others, in these words: "Behold my servant whom I have chosen," etc., Isa. xliii. 10. Which place is alleged by St. Matthew as fulfilled now in Christ, Matt. xii. 18. Wherein is propounded—
First, the calling of Christ to his office.
Secondly, the execution of it.

I. For his calling: God styleth him here his righteous servant, etc. Christ was God's servant in the greatest piece of service that ever was; a chosen, and a choice servant: he did and suffered all by commission from the Father: wherein we may see the sweet love of God to us, that counts the work of our salvation by Christ his greatest service; and that he will put his only beloved Son to that service. He might well prefix *Behold*, to raise up our thoughts to the highest pitch of attention and admiration. In time of temptation, misgiving consciences look so much to the present trouble they are in, that they need be roused up to behold him in whom they may find rest for their distressed souls. In temptations it is safest to behold nothing but Christ the true brazen Serpent, the true *Lamb of God that taketh away the sins of the world*, John i. 29. This saving object hath a special influence of comfort into the soul, especially if we look not only on Christ, but upon the Father's authority and love in him. For in all that Christ did and suffered as Mediator, we must see *God in him reconciling the world unto himself*, 2 Cor. v. 19.

What a support to our faith is this, that God the Father, the party offended by our sins, is so well pleased with the work of redemption! And what a comfort is this, that seeing God's love resteth on Christ, as well pleased in him, we may gather that he is as well pleased with us, if we be in Christ! For his love resteth in whole Christ, in Christ mystical as well as Christ natural, because he loveth him and us with one love. Let us, therefore, embrace Christ, and in him God's love, and build our faith safely on such a Saviour, that is furnished with so high a commission.

See here, for our comfort, a sweet agreement of all three persons: the Father giveth a commission to Christ; the Spirit furnisheth and sanctifieth to it; Christ himself executeth the office of a Mediator. Our redemption is founded upon the joint agreement of all three persons of the Trinity.

II. For the execution of this his calling, it is set down here to be modest, without making a noise, or raising dust by any pompous coming, as princes use to do. "*His voice shall not be heard.*" His voice indeed was heard, but what voice? "*Come unto me, all ye that are weary and heavy laden,*" Matt. xi. 28. He cried, but how? "*Ho, every one that thirsteth, come,*" etc., Isa. lv. 1. And as his coming was modest, so it was mild, which is set down in these words : The bruised reed shall he not break, etc.　Wherein we may observe these three things :—

First, The condition of those that Christ had to deal withal.　(1.) They were *bruised reeds ;* (2.) *smoking flax*.

Secondly, Christ's carriage toward them.　He *brake not* the bruised reed, nor *quenched* the smoking flax : where more is meant than spoken ; for he will not only not break the bruised reed, nor quench, etc., but he will cherish them.

Thirdly, The constancy and progress of this his tender care, "*until judgment come to victory*"— that is, until the sanctified frame of grace begun in their hearts be brought to that perfection, that it prevaileth over all opposite corruption.

1. For the *first*, the condition of men whom he was to deal withal is, that they were bruised reeds, and smoking flax ; not trees, but reeds ; and not whole, but bruised reeds.　The Church is compared to weak things ; to a dove amongst the fowls ; to a vine amongst the plants ; to sheep amongst the beasts ; to a woman, which is the weaker vessel : and here God's children are compared to bruised reeds and smoking flax.　First, we will speak of them as they are bruised reeds, and then as smoking flax.

They are bruised reeds before their conversion, and oftentimes after: before conversion all (except such as being bred up in the church, God hath delighted to shew himself gracious unto from their childhood), yet in different degrees, as God seeth meet; and as difference is in regard of temper, parts, manner of life, etc., so in God's intendment of employment for the time to come; for usually he empties such of themselves, and makes them nothing, before he will use them in any great services.

(1.) This bruised reed is a man that for the most part is in some misery, as those were that came to Christ for help, and (2.) by misery is brought to see sin the cause of it; for whatsoever pretences sin maketh, yet bruising or breaking is the end of it; (3.) he is sensible of sin and misery, even unto bruising; and (4.) seeing no help in himself, is carried with restless desire to have supply from another, with some hope, which a little raiseth him out of himself to Christ, though he dareth not claim any present interest of mercy. This spark of hope being opposed by doubtings, and fears rising from corruption, maketh him as smoking flax; so that both these together, a *bruised* reed and *smoking* flax, make up the state of a poor distressed man. Such an

one as our Saviour Christ termeth poor in spirit,
Matt. v. 3, who seeth a want, and withal seeth
himself indebted to divine justice, and no means
of supply from himself or the creature, and
thereupon mourns, and upon some hope of mercy
from the promise and examples of those that
have obtained mercy, is stirred up to hunger and
thirst after it.

CHAP. II.—*Those that Christ hath to do withal are bruised.*

This bruising is required [1.] before conversion,
(1.) that so the Spirit may make way for itself
into the heart by levelling all proud, high
thoughts, and that we may understand ourselves to be what indeed we are by nature. We
love to wander from ourselves and to be strangers
at home, till God bruiseth us by one cross or
other, and then we *bethink ourselves*, and come
home to ourselves with the prodigal, Luke xv. 17.
A marvellous hard thing it is to bring a dull
and a shifting heart to cry with feeling for mercy.
Our hearts, like malefactors, until they be beaten
from all shifts, never cry for the mercy of the
Judge. Again (2.) this bruising maketh us set a
high price upon Christ. The gospel is the gospel

indeed then; then the fig-leaves of morality will do us no good. And (3.) it maketh us more thankful, and (4.) from thankfulness more fruitful in our lives; for what maketh many so cold and barren, but that bruising for sin never endeared God's grace unto them? Likewise (5.) this dealing of God doth establish us the more in his ways, having had knocks and bruisings in our own ways. This is the cause oft of relapses and apostasies, because men never smarted for sin at the first; they were not long enough under the lash of the law. Hence this inferior work of the Spirit, in *bringing down high thoughts*, 2 Cor. x. 5, is necessary before conversion. And, for the most part, the Holy Spirit, to further the work of conviction, joineth some affliction, which, sanctified, hath a healing and purging power.

Nay, [2.] after conversion we need bruising, that (1.) reeds may know themselves to be reeds, and not oaks; even reeds need bruising, by reason of the remainder of pride in our nature, and to let us see that we live by mercy. And (2.) that weaker Christians may not be too much discouraged when they see stronger shaken and bruised. Thus Peter was bruised when he wept bitterly, Matt. xxvi. 75. This reed, till he met with this bruise, had more wind in him than pith.

" Though all forsake thee, I will not," etc., Matt. xxvi. 35.   The people of God cannot be without these examples.   The heroical deeds of those great worthies do not comfort the church so much as their falls and bruises do.   Thus David was bruised, Ps. xxxii. 3-5, until he came to a free confession, without guile of spirit ; nay, his sorrows did rise in his own feeling unto the exquisite pain of breaking of bones, Ps. li. 8.   Thus Hezekiah complains that God had " broken his bones " as a lion, Isa. xxxvii. 13.   Thus the chosen vessel St. Paul needed the messenger of Satan to buffet him, lest he should be lifted up above measure, 2 Cor. xii. 7.

Hence we learn that we must not pass too harsh judgment upon ourselves or others when God doth exercise us with bruising upon bruising ; there must be a conformity to our head, Christ, who " was bruised for us," Isa. liii. 5, that we may know how much we are bound unto him.   Profane spirits, ignorant of God's ways in bringing his children to heaven, censure broken-hearted Christians for desperate persons, whenas God is about a gracious good work with them.   It is no easy matter to bring a man from nature to grace, and from grace to glory, so unyielding and untractable are our hearts.

CHAP. III.—*Christ will not break the Bruised Reed.*

2. The second point is, that Christ will not "*break the bruised reed.*" Physicians, though they put their patients to much pain, yet they will not destroy nature, but raise it up by degrees. Chirurgeons will lance and cut, but not dismember. A mother that hath a sick and froward child will not therefore cast it away. And shall there be more mercy in the stream than in the spring? Shall we think there is more mercy in ourselves than in God, who planteth the affection of mercy in us? But for further declaration of Christ's mercy to all bruised reeds, consider the comfortable relations he hath taken upon him of husband, shepherd, brother, etc., which he will discharge to the utmost; for shall others by his grace fulfil what he calleth them unto, and not he that, out of his love, hath taken upon him these relations, so thoroughly founded upon his Father's assignment, and his own voluntary undertaking? Consider his borrowed names from the mildest creatures, as lamb, hen, etc., to shew his tender care; consider his very name, Jesus, a Saviour, given him by God himself; consider his office, answerable to his name, which

is that he should "heal the broken-hearted,"
Isa. lxi. 1.   At his baptism the Holy Ghost sate
on him in the shape of a dove, to shew that he
should be a dove-like, gentle Mediator.   See the
gracious manner of executing his offices.   As a
prophet, he came with blessing in his mouth,
"Blessed be the poor in spirit," etc., Matt. v. 3,
and invited those to come to him, whose hearts
suggested most exceptions against themselves,
"Come unto me, all ye that are weary and
heavy laden," Matt. xi. 28.   How did his bowels
yearn when "he saw the people as sheep without
a shepherd!" Matt. ix. 36.   He never turned any
back again that came unto him, though some
went away of themselves.   He came to die as a
priest for his enemies.   In the days of his flesh
he dictated a form of prayer unto his disciples,
and put petitions unto God into their mouths,
and his Spirit to intercede in their hearts; and
now makes intercession in heaven for weak
Christians, standing between God's anger and
them; and shed tears for those that shed his
blood.   So he is a meek King; he will admit
mourners into his presence, a king of poor and
afflicted persons: as he hath beams of majesty,
so he hath bowels of mercies and compassion;
"A prince of peace," Isa. ix. 6.   Why was he

"tempted," but "that he might succour those that are tempted," Heb. ii. 18. What mercy may we not expect from so gracious a Mediator, 1 Tim. ii. 5, that took our nature upon him that he might be gracious. He is a physician good at all diseases, especially at the binding up of a broken heart; he died that he might heal our souls with a plaster of his own blood, and by that death save us, which we were the procurers of ourselves, by our own sins; and hath he not the same bowels in heaven? "Saul, Saul, why persecutest thou me?" Acts ix. 4, cried the head in heaven, when the foot was trodden on, on earth. His advancement hath not made him forget his own flesh; though it has freed him from passion, yet not from compassion towards us. The lion of the tribe of Judah will only tear in pieces those that "will not have him rule over them," Luke xix. 17. He will not shew his strength against those that prostrate themselves before him.

Use 1. What should we learn from hence, but "to come boldly to the throne of grace," Heb. iv. 16, in all our grievances? Shall our sins discourage us, when he appears there only for sinners? Art thou bruised? Be of good comfort, he calleth thee; conceal not thy wounds,

open all before him, keep not Satan's counsel.
Go to Christ though trembling; as the poor
woman, if we can but "touch the hem of his
garment," Matt. ix. 20, we shall be healed and
have a gracious answer. Go boldly to God in
our flesh; for this end that we might go boldly
to him, he is flesh of our flesh, and bone of our
bone.. Never fear to go to God, since we have
such a Mediator with him, that is not only our
friend, but our brother and husband. Well
might the angels proclaim from heaven, " Behold,
we bring you tidings of joy," Luke ii. 10. Well
might the apostle stir us up to "rejoice in the
Lord again and again," Phil. iv. 4 : he was well
advised upon what grounds he did it. Peace and
joy are two main fruits of his kingdom. Let the
world be as it will, if we cannot rejoice in the
world, yet we may rejoice in the Lord. His
presence maketh any condition comfortable.
" Be not afraid," saith he to his disciples, when
they were afraid, as if they had seen a ghost,
" It is I," Matt. xiv. 27 ; as if there were no cause
of fear where he is present.

Use 2. Let this stay us when we feel ourselves
bruised. Christ's course is first to wound, then
to heal. No sound, whole soul shall ever enter
into heaven. Think in temptation, Christ was

tempted for me ; according to my trials will be my graces and comforts. If Christ be so merciful as not to break me, I will not break myself by despair, nor yield myself over to the roaring lion Satan, to break me in pieces.

Use. 3. Thirdly, See the contrary disposition of Christ, and Satan and his instruments. Satan setteth upon us when we are weakest, as Simeon and Levi upon the " Shechemites, when they were sore," Gen. xxxiv. 25 ; but Christ will make up in us all the breaches sin and Satan have made ; he "binds up the broken-hearted," Isa. lxi. 1. And as a mother tendereth most the most diseased and weakest child, so doth Christ most mercifully incline to the weakest, and likewise putteth an instinct into the weakest things to rely upon something stronger than themselves for support. The vine stayeth itself upon the elm, and the weakest creatures have oft the strongest shelters. The consciousness of the Church's weakness makes her willing to lean on her beloved, and to hide herself under his wing.

CHAP. IV.—*Signs of one truly bruised. Means and measure of bruising, and comfort to such.*

Objection. But how shall we know whether we are such as those that may expect mercy?

Answer 1. By bruising here is not meant those that are brought low only by crosses, but such as by them are brought to see their sin, which bruiseth most of all. When conscience is under the guilt of sin, then every judgment brings a report of God's anger to the soul, and all less troubles run into this great trouble of conscience for sin. As all corrupt humours run to the diseased and bruised part of the body, and as every creditor falls upon the debtor when he is once arrested, so when conscience is once awaked, all former sins and present crosses join together to make the bruise the more painful. Now, he that is thus bruised will be content with nothing but with mercy from him that hath bruised him. "He hath wounded, and he must heal," Isa. lxi. 1. Lord, thou hast bruised me deservedly for my sins, bind up my heart again, etc. 2. Again a man truly bruised, judgeth sin the greatest evil, and the favour of God the greatest good. 3. He had rather hear of mercy than of a kingdom. 4. He hath mean conceits of himself, and thinketh he is not worth the earth he treads on. 5. Towards others he is not censorious, as being taken up at home, but is full of sympathy and compassion to those that are under God's hand. 6. He thinketh those that walk in the comforts of God's Spirit the happiest men of the world. 7. "He trembleth at the word of God," Isa. lxvi. 2, and honoureth the very feet of those blessed instruments that bring peace unto him, Rom. x. 15. 8. He is more taken up with the inward exercises of a broken heart than with formality, and yet careful to use all sanctified means to convey comfort.

Question. But how shall we come to have this temper?

Answer. First, we must conceive of bruising either as a state into which God bringeth us, or as a duty to be performed by us. Both are here meant. We must join with God in bruising of ourselves. When he humbles us, let us humble ourselves, and not stand out against him, for then he will redouble his strokes; and let us justify Christ in all his chastisements, knowing that all his dealing towards us is to cause us to return into our own hearts. His work in bruising tendeth to our work in bruising ourselves. Let us lament our own untowardness, and say, Lord, what a heart have I that needs all this, that none of this could be spared ! We must lay siege to the hardness of our own hearts, and aggravate sin all we can. We must look on Christ, who was bruised for us, look on him whom we have pierced with our sins. But all directions will not prevail, unless God by his Spirit convinceth us deeply, setting our sins before us, and driving us to a stand. Then we will make out for mercy. Conviction will breed contrition, and this humilia-·tion. Therefore desire God that he would bring a clear and a strong light into all the corners of our souls, and accompany it with a spirit of power to lay our hearts low.

A set measure of bruising ourselves cannot be prescribed; yet it must be so far, as (1.) we may prize Christ above all, and see that a Saviour must be had ; and (2.) until we reform that which is amiss, though it be to the cutting off our right hand, or pulling out our right eye. There is a dangerous slighting of the work of humiliation, some alleging this for a pretence for their overly dealing with their own hearts, that Christ will not break the bruised reed ; but such must know that every sudden terror and short grief is not that which makes us bruised reeds ; not a *little hanging down our heads like a bulrush*, Isa. lviii. 5, but a working our hearts to such a grief as will make sin more odious unto us than punishment, until we offer a holy violence against it; else, favouring ourselves, we make work for God to bruise us, and for sharp repentance afterwards. It is dangerous, I confess, in some cases with some spirits, to press too much and too long this bruising, because they may die under the wound and burden before they be raised up again. Therefore it is good in mixed assemblies to mingle comfort, that every soul may have its due portion. But if we lay this for a ground, that there is more mercy in Christ than sin in us, there can be no danger in thorough dealing. It is better to go bruised to heaven than sound to hell. Therefore let us not take off ourselves too soon, nor pull off the plaster before the cure be wrought, but keep ourselves under this work till sin be the sourest, and Christ the sweetest, of all things. And when God's hand is upon us in any kind, it is good to divert our sorrow for other things to the root of all, which is sin. Let our grief run most in that channel, that as sin bred grief, so grief may consume sin.

Quest. But are we not bruised unless we grieve more for sin than we do for punishment?

Ans. Sometimes our grief from outward grievances may lie heavier upon the soul than grief for God's displeasure ; because in such cases the grief works upon the whole man, both outward and inward, and hath nothing to stay it, but a little spark of faith : which, by reason of the violent impression of the grievance, is suspended in the exercises of it : and this is most felt in sudden distresses which come upon the soul as a torrent or land-flood, and especially in bodily distempers, which, by reason of the sympathy between the soul and the body, work upon the soul so far as they hinder not only the spiritual, but often the natural acts.   Hereupon St. James wisheth in affliction to pray ourselves, but in case of sickness to *send for the elders*, James v. 14 ; that may, as those in the gospel, offer up the sick person to God in their prayers, being unable to present their own case.   Hereupon God admitteth of such a plea from the sharpness and bitterness of the grievance, as in David, Ps. vi., etc.   "The Lord knoweth whereof we are made, he remembereth we are but dust," Ps. ciii. 14 ; that our strength is not the strength of steel.   It is a branch of his faithfulness unto us as his creatures, whence he is called "a faithful Creator," 1 Pet. iv. 19 ; "God is faithful, who will not suffer us to be tempted above that we are able," 1 Cor. x. 13. There were certain commandments which the Jews called the hedges of the law: as to fence men off from cruelty, he commanded they should "not take the dam with the young, nor seethe the kid in the mother's milk," Exod. xxiii. 19; "nor muzzle the mouth of the ox," 1 Cor. ix. 9. Hath God care of beasts, and not of his more noble creature? And therefore we ought to judge charitably of the complaints of God's people which are wrung from them in such cases. Job had the esteem with God of a patient man, notwithstanding those passionate complaints. Faith overborne for the present will get ground again; and grief for sin, although it come short of grief for misery in violence, yet it goeth beyond it in constancy; as a running stream fed with a spring holdeth out, when a sudden swelling brook faileth.

For the concluding of this point, and our encouragement to a thorough work of bruising, and patience under God's bruising of us, let all know that none are fitter for comfort than those that think themselves furthest off. Men, for the most part, are not lost enough in their own feeling for a Saviour. A holy despair in ourselves is the ground of true hope, Hos. xiv. 3. In God the fatherless find mercy: if men were more fatherless, they should feel more God's fatherly affection from heaven; for God that dwelleth in highest heavens, Isa. lxvi. 2, dwelleth likewise in the lowest soul. Christ's sheep are weak sheep, and wanting in something or other; he therefore applieth himself to the necessities of every sheep. "He seeks that which was lost, and brings again that which was driven out of the way, and binds up that which was broken, and strengthens the weak," Ezek. xxxiv. 16; his tenderest care is over the weakest. The lambs he carrieth in his bosom, Isa. xl. 11; "Peter, feed my lambs," John xxi. 15. He was most familiar and open to the troubled souls. How careful was he that Peter and the rest of the apostles should not be too much dejected after his resurrection! "Go tell the disciples, and tell Peter," Mark xvi. 7. Christ knew that guilt of their unkindness in leaving of him had dejected their spirits. How gently did he endure Thomas' unbelief! and stooped so far unto his weakness as to suffer him to thrust his hand into his side.

CHAP. V.—*Grace is little at first.*

For the second branch, God will not quench the smoking flax, or wick, but will blow it up till it flameth. In smoking flax there is but a little light, and that weak, as being not able to flame, and this little mixed with smoke.

The observations hence are, first, *That in God's children, especially in their first conversion, there is but a little measure of grace, and that little mixed with much corruption, which, as smoke, is offensive.* Secondly, *That Christ will not quench this smoking flax.*

Obs. 1. For the first, *Grace is little at the first.* There are several ages in Christians, some babes, some young men : grace is as "a grain of mustard seed," Matt. xvii. 20. Nothing so little as grace at first, and nothing more glorious afterward : things of greatest perfection are longest in coming to their growth. Man, the perfectest creature, comes to perfection by little and little ; worthless things, as mushrooms and the like, like Jonah's gourd, soon spring up, and soon vanish. A new creature is the most excellent frame in all the world, therefore it groweth up by degrees ; we see in nature that a mighty oak riseth of an acorn. It is with a Christian as it was with Christ, who sprang out of the dead stock of Jesse, out of David's family, Isa. liii. 2, when it was at the lowest, but he grew up higher than the heavens. It is not with the trees of righteousness as it was with the trees of paradise, which were created all perfect at the first. The seeds of all the creatures in this goodly frame of the world were hid in the chaos, in that confused mass at the first, out of which God did command all creatures to arise ; in the small seeds of plants lie hid both bulk and branches, bud and fruit. In a few principles lie hid all comfortable conclusions of holy truth. All these glorious fireworks of zeal and holiness in the saints had their beginning from a few sparks.

Let us not therefore be discouraged at the small beginnings of grace, but look on ourselves as "elected to be blameless and without spot," Eph. i. 4. Let us only look on our imperfect beginning to enforce further strife to perfection, and to keep us in a low conceit. Otherwise, in case of discouragement, we must consider ourselves, as Christ doth, who looks on us as such as he intendeth to fit for himself. Christ valueth us by what we shall be, and by that we are elected unto. We call a little plant a tree, because it is growing up to be so. "Who is he that despiseth the day of little things?" Zech. iv. 10. Christ would not have us despise little things.

The glorious angels disdain not attendance on little ones; little in their own eyes, and little in the eyes of the world.

Grace, though little in quantity, yet is much in vigour and worth.

It is Christ that raiseth the worth of little and mean places and persons. Bethlehem the least, Micah v. 2, Matt. ii. 6, and yet not the least; the least in itself, not the least in respect Christ was born there. The second temple, Hag. ii. 9, came short of the outward magnificence of the former; yet more glorious than the first, because Christ came into it. The Lord of the temple came into his own temple. The pupil of the eye is very little, yet seeth a great part of the heaven at once. A pearl, though little, yet is of much esteem: nothing in the world of so good use, as the least dram of grace.

CHAP. VI.—*Grace is mingled with Corruption.*

Obs. 2. But grace is not only little, but mingled with corruption; whereof it is, that a Christian is said to be smoking flax. Whence we see, that *grace doth not waste corruption all at once, but some is left to conflict withal.* The purest actions of the purest men need Christ to perfume them, and so is his office. When we pray, we need to pray again for Christ to pardon the defects of them. See some instances of this smoking flax. Moses at the Red Sea, being in a great perplexity, and knowing not what to say, or which way to turn him, groaned to God: no doubt this was a great conflict in him. In great distresses we know not what to pray, but the Spirit makes request with sighs that cannot be expressed, Rom. viii. 26. Broken hearts can yield but broken prayers.

When David was before the king of Gath, 1 Sam. xxi. 13, and disfigured himself in an uncomely manner, in that smoke there was some fire also; you may see what an excellent psalm he makes upon that occasion, Ps. xxxiv.; wherein, upon experience, ver. 18, he saith, "The Lord is near unto them that are of a contrite spirit;" Ps. xxxi. 22, "I said in my haste, I am cast out of thy sight;" there is smoke: "yet thou heardest the voice of my prayer;" there is fire. "Master, carest thou not that we perish?" Matt. viii. 25, cry the disciples; here is smoke of infidelity, yet so much light of faith as stirred them up to pray to Christ. "Lord, I believe:" there is light; "but help my unbelief," Mark ix. 24: there is smoke.

Jonah cries, ii. 4, "I am cast out of thy sight :" there is smoke; "yet will I look again to thy holy temple :" there is light.

"O miserable man that I am," Rom. vii. 24, saith St. Paul upon sense of his corruption ; but yet breaks out into thanks to God through Jesus Christ our Lord.

"I sleep," saith the Church in the Canticles, "but my heart wakes," Cant. v. 2. In the seven Churches, which for their light are called, "seven golden candlesticks," Rev. ii., iii., most of them had much smoke with their light.

The ground of this mixture is, that we carry about us a double principle, grace and nature. The end of it is especially to preserve us from those two dangerous rocks which our natures are prone to dash upon, security and pride ; and to force us to pitch our rest on justification, not sanctification, which, besides imperfection, hath some soil.

Our spiritual fire is like our ordinary fire here below, that is, mixed ; but fire is most pure in its own element above ; so shall all our graces be when we are where we would be, in heaven, which is our proper element.

Use. From this mixture it is, that the people of God have so different judgments of themselves, looking sometimes at the work of grace, sometimes at the remainder of corruption, and when they look upon that, then they think they have no grace ; though they love Christ in his ordinances and children, yet dare not challenge so near acquaintance as to be his. Even as a candle in the socket sometimes sheweth its light, and sometimes the shew of light is lost ; so sometimes well persuaded they are of themselves, sometimes at a loss.

Chap. VII.—*Christ will not quench small and weak beginnings.*

Doct. Now for the second observation, *Christ will not quench the smoking flax.* First, because this spark is from heaven, it is his own, it is kindled by his own Spirit. And secondly, it tendeth to the glory of his powerful grace in his children, that he preserveth light in the midst of darkness,—a spark in the midst of the swelling waters of corruption.

There is an especial blessing in that little spark ; "when wine is found in a cluster, one saith, Destroy it not ; for there is a blessing in it,"

Isa. lxv. 8. We see how our Saviour Christ bore with Thomas in his doubting, John xx. 27 ; with the two disciples that went to Emmaus, who staggered "whether he came to redeem Israel or no," Luke xxiv. 21 : he quenched not that little light in Peter which was smothered : Peter denied him, but he denied not Peter, Matt. xxvi. "If thou wilt, thou canst," said one poor man in the gospel, Matt. viii. 2 ; "Lord, if thou canst," said another, Mark ix. 22 ; both were this smoking flax, neither of both were quenched. If Christ had stood upon his own greatness, he would have rejected him that came with his *if ;* but Christ answers his *if* with a gracious and absolute grant, "I will, be thou clean." The woman that was diseased with an issue did but touch, and with a trembling hand, and but the hem of his garment, and yet went away both healed and comforted. In the seven churches, Rev. ii., iii., we see he acknowledgeth and cherisheth anything that was good in them. Because the disciples slept of infirmity, being oppressed with grief, our Saviour Christ frameth a comfortable excuse for them, "The spirit is willing, but the flesh is weak," Matt. xxvi. 41.

If Christ should not be merciful, he would miss of his own ends ; "there is mercy with thee that thou mayst be feared," Ps. cxxx. 4. Now all are willing to come under that banner of love which he spreadeth over his: "therefore to thee shall all flesh come," Ps. lxv. 2. He useth moderation and care, "lest the spirit should fail before him, and the souls which he hath made," Isa. lvii. 16. Christ's heart yearned, the text saith, "when he saw them without meat, lest they should faint," Matt. xv. 32 ; much more will he have regard for the preventing of our spiritual faintings.

Here see the opposite disposition between the holy nature of Christ, and the impure nature of man. Man for a little smoke will quench the light ; Christ ever we see cherisheth even the least beginnings. How bare he with the many imperfections of his poor disciples. If he did sharply check them, it was in love, and that they might shine the brighter. Can we have a better pattern to follow than this of him by whom we hope to be saved ? "We that are strong ought to bear with the infirmities of them that are weak," Rom. xv. 1. "I become all things to all men, that I may win some," 1 Cor. ix. 22. Oh, that this gaining and winning disposition were more in many ! Many, so far as in us lieth, are lost for want of encouragement. See how that faithful fisher of men, St. Paul, labours to catch his judge, " I know thou believest the prophets," Acts xxvi. 27 ; and then wisheth all saving good, but not bonds ; he might have added them too, but he would not discourage one that made but an offer, he would therefore wish Agrippa only that which was good in religion. How careful was our blessed Saviour of little ones that they might not be offended, Matt. xii., xiii. How doth he defend his disciples from malicious imputations of the Pharisees ! How careful not to put new wine into old vessels, Matt. ix. 17, not to alienate new beginners with the austerities of religion (as some indiscreetly). Oh, saith he, they shall have time to fast when I am gone, and strength to fast when the Holy Ghost is come upon them.

It is not the best way to fall foul presently with young beginners for some lesser vanities, but shew them a more excellent way, and breed them up in positive grounds, and other things will be quickly out of credit with them. It is not amiss to conceal their wants, to excuse some failings, to commend their performances, to cherish their towardness, to remove all rubs out of their way, to help them every way to bear the yoke of religion with greater ease, to bring them in love with God and his service, lest they distaste it before they know it. For the most part we see Christ planteth in young beginners a love which we call "the first love," Rev. ii. 4, to carry them through their profession with more delight, and doth not expose them to crosses before they have gathered strength; as we breed up young plants, and fence them from the weather, until they be rooted. Mercy to others should move us to deny ourselves in our lawful liberties oftentimes, in case of offence of weak ones; it is the "little ones that are offended," Matt. xviii. 6. The weakest are aptest to think themselves despised, therefore we should be most careful to give them content.

It were a good strife amongst Christians, one to labour to give no offence, and the other to labour to take none. The best men are severe to themselves, tender over others.

Yet people should not tire and wear out the patience of others: nor should the weaker so far exact moderation from others, as to bear out themselves upon their indulgence, and so to rest in their own infirmities, with danger to their own souls, and scandal to the church.

Neither hereupon must they set light by the gifts of God in others, which grace teacheth to honour wheresoever they are found, but know their parts and place, and not enterprise anything above their measure, which may make their persons and their case obnoxious to scorn. When blindness and boldness, ignorance and arrogance, weakness and wilfulness meet together in one, it renders men odious to God, it maketh men burdensome in society, dangerous in their counsels, troublers of better designs, untractable and incapable of better direction, miserable in the issue: where Christ sheweth his gracious power in weakness, he doth it by letting men understand themselves so far as to breed humility, and magnifying of God's love to such as they are: he doth it as a preservative against discouragements from weakness, seeing it bringeth men into a less distance from grace, as being an advantage to poverty of spirit, than greatness of condition and parts, which yield to corrupt nature fuel for pride. Christ refuseth none for weakness of parts, that none should be discouraged; accepteth of none for greatness, that none should be lifted up with that which is of so little reckoning with God. It is no great matter how dull the scholar be, when Christ taketh upon him to be the teacher: who as he prescribeth what to understand, so he giveth understanding itself even to the simplest.

The Church suffereth much from weak ones, therefore we may challenge liberty to deal with them, as mildly, so oftentimes directly. The scope of true love is to make the party better, which by concealment oftentimes is hindered; with some a spirit of meekness prevaileth most, but with some a rod. Some must be "pulled out of the fire," Jude 23, with violence, and they will bless God for us in the day of their visitation. We see our Saviour multiplies woe upon woe when he was to deal with hard-hearted hypocrites, Matt. xxiii. 13, for hypocrites' need stronger conviction than gross sinners, because their will is nought, and thereupon usually their conversion is violent. A hard knot must have an answerable wedge, else in a cruel pity we betray their souls. A sharp reproof sometimes is a precious pearl, and a sweet balm. The wounds of secure sinners will not be healed with sweet words. The Holy Ghost came as well in fiery tongues as in the likeness of a dove, and the same Holy Spirit will vouchsafe a spirit of prudence and discretion, which is the salt to season all our words and actions. And such wisdom will teach us "to speak a word in season," Isa. l. 4, both to the weary, and likewise to the secure soul. And, indeed, he had need have "the tongue of the learned," Isa. l. 4, that shall either raise up or cast down ; but in this place I speak of mildness towards those that are weak and are sensible of it. These we must bring on gently, and drive softly, as Jacob did his cattle, Gen. xxxiii. 14, according to their pace, and as his children were able to endure.

Weak Christians are like glasses which are hurt with the least violent usage, otherwise if gently handled will continue a long time. This honour of gentle use we are to "give to the weaker vessels," 1 Pet. iii. 7, by which we shall both preserve them, and likewise make them useful to the church and ourselves.

In unclean bodies if all ill humours be purged out, you shall purge life and all away. Therefore though God saith, that "he will fine them as silver is fined," Zech. xiii. 9 ; yet, Isa. xlviii. 10, he said, "he hath fined them, but not as silver," that is, so exactly as that no dross remaineth, for he hath respect to our weakness. Perfect refining is for another world, for the world of the souls of perfect men.

CHAP. VIII.—*Tenderness required in Ministers toward young Beginners.*

1. Divines had need to take heed therefore how they deal with these in divers particulars: as first let them be careful they strain not things too high, making those general and necessary evidences of grace, which agree not to the experience of many a good Christian, and lay salvation and damnation upon those things that are not fit to bear so great a weight, whereupon men are groundlessly cast down lower by them, than they can hastily be raised up again by themselves or others. The ambassadors of so gentle a Saviour should not be over-masterly, setting up themselves in the hearts of people where Christ alone should sit as in his own temple. Too much respect to man was one of the inlets of popery. "Let a man account of us as of the ministers of Christ," 1 Cor. iv. 1, neither more nor less, just so much. How careful was St. Paul in cases of conscience not to lay a snare upon any weak conscience.

They should take heed likewise that they hide not their meaning in dark speeches, speaking in the clouds. Truth feareth nothing so much as concealment, and desireth nothing so much as clearly to be laid open to the view of all : when it is most naked, it is most lovely and powerful.

Our blessed Saviour, as he took our nature upon him, so he took upon him our familiar manner of speech, which was part of his voluntary abasement. St. Paul was a profound man, yet became as a nurse to the weaker sort, 1. Thess. ii. 7.

That spirit of mercy that was in Christ should move his servants to be content to abase themselves for the good of the meanest. What made the "kingdom of heaven suffer violence," Matt. xi. 22, after John the Baptist's time, but that comfortable truths were with that plainness and evidence laid open, that the people were so affected with them, as they offered a holy violence to them ?

Christ chose those to preach mercy, which had felt most mercy, as St. Peter and St. Paul ; that they might be examples of what they taught. St. Paul "became all things to all men," 1 Cor. ix. 2, stooping unto them for their good. Christ came down from heaven, and emptied himself of majesty in tender love to souls; shall we not come down from our high conceits to do any poor soul good? shall man be proud after God hath been humble ? We see the ministers of

Satan turn themselves into all shapes to "make proselytes," Matt. xxiii. 15. A Jesuit will be every man. We see ambitious men study accommodation of themselves to the humours of those by whom they hope to be raised ; and shall not we study application of ourselves to Christ, by whom we hope to be advanced, nay, are already sitting with him in heavenly places ? After we are gained to Christ ourselves, we should labour to gain others to Christ. Holy ambition and covetousness will move us to put upon ourselves the disposition of Christ : but we must put off ourselves first.

We should not, thirdly, rack their wits with curious or "doubtful disputes," Rom. xiv. 1 ; for so we shall distract and tire them, and give occasion to make them cast off the care of all. That age of the Church which was most fertile in nice questions, was most barren in religion : for it makes people think religion to be only a matter of wit, in tying and untying of knots ; the brains of men given that way are hotter usually than their hearts.

Yet, notwithstanding, when we are cast into times and places wherein doubts are raised about main points, here people ought to labour to be established. God suffereth questions oftentimes to arise for trial of our love and exercise of our parts. Nothing is so certain as that which is certain after doubts. *Nil tam certum quâm quod ex dubio certum.* Shaking settles and roots. In a contentious age, it is a witty thing to be a Christian, and to know what to pitch their souls upon ; it is an office of love here to take away the stones, and to smooth the way to heaven. Therefore, we must take heed that, under pretence of avoidance of disputes, we do not suffer an adverse party to get ground upon the truth ; for thus may we easily betray both the truth of God and souls of men.

And likewise those are failing that, by overmuch austerity, drive back troubled souls from having comfort by them ; for by this carriage many smother their temptations, and burn inwardly, because they have none into whose bosom they may vent their grief and ease their souls.

We must neither bind where God looseth, nor loose where God bindeth, nor open where God shutteth, nor shut where God openeth ; the right use of the keys is always successful. In personal application there must be great heed taken ; for a man may be a false prophet, and yet speak the truth. If it be not a truth to the person to

whom he speaketh; if he "grieve those whom
God hath not grieved," Lam. iii. 33, by unseasonable truths, or by comforts in an ill way, the
hearts of the wicked may be strengthened. One
man's meat may be another's bane.

If we look to the general temper of these
times, rousing and waking Scriptures are fittest;
yet there be many broken spirits need soft and
oily words. Even in the worst time the prophets mingled sweet comfort for the hidden rem-
nant of faithful people. God hath comfort;
"Comfort ye my people," Isa. xl. 1, as well as
"lift up thy voice as a trumpet," Isa. lviii. 1.

And here likewise there needs a caveat.
Mercy doth not rob us of our right judgment,
as that we should take stinking fire-brands for
smoking flax. None will claim mercy more of
others, than those whose portion is due severity.
This example doth not countenance lukewarm-
ness, nor too much indulgence to those that
need quickening. Cold diseases must have hot
remedies. It made for the just commendations
of the Church of Ephesus, "that it could not
bear with them which are evil," Rev. ii. 2. We
should so bear with others, as we discover withal
a dislike of evil. Our Saviour Christ would not
forbear sharp reproof where he saw dangerous

infirmities in his most beloved disciples. · It bringeth under a curse "to do the work of the Lord negligently," Jer. xlviii. 10; even where it is a work of just severity, as when it is sheathing the sword in the bowels of the enemy. And those whom we suffer to be betrayed by their worst enemies, their sins, will have just cause to curse us another day.

It is hard to preserve just bounds of mercy and severity, without a spirit above our own; which we ought to desire to be led withal in all things. That "wisdom which dwelleth with prudence," Prov. viii. 12, will guide us in these particulars, without which virtue is not ·virtue, truth not truth. The rule and the case must be laid together; for if there be not a narrow insight, seeming likeness in conditions will be the breeder of errors in our opinions of them. Those fiery, tempestuous, and destructive spirits in popery, that seek to promote their religion by cruelty, shew that they are strangers to that wisdom which is from above, which maketh men gentle, peaceable, and ready to shew that mercy they have]felt before themselves. It is a way of prevailing, as agreeablé to Christ, so likewise to man's nature, to prevail by some forbearance and moderation.

And yet oft we see a false spirit in those that call for moderation. It is but to carry their own projects with the greater strength ; and if they prove of the prevailing hand, they will hardly show that moderation to others they now call for from others. And there is a proud kind of moderation likewise, when men will take upon them to censure both parties, as if they were wiser than both, although, if the spirit be right, a looker on may see more than those that are in conflict.

CHAP. IX.—*Governors should be tender of weak ones, and also private Christians.*

2. So in the censures of the church, it is more suitable to the spirit of Christ to incline to the milder part, and not to kill a fly on the forehead with a beetle, nor shut men out of heaven for a trifle. The very snuffers of the tabernacle were made of pure gold, to shew the purity of those censures, whereby the light of the church is kept bright. That power that is given to the church is given for edification, not destruction. How careful was St. Paul, that the incestuous Corinthian, 2 Cor. ii. 7, repenting, should not be swallowed up with too much grief.

As for civil magistrates, they, for civil exigencies and reasons of state, must let the law have its course; yet thus far they should imitate this mild king, as not to mingle bitterness and passion with authority derived from God. Authority is a beam of God's majesty, and prevaileth most where there is least mixture of that which is man's. It requireth more than ordinary wisdom to manage it aright. This string must not be too much strained up, nor too much let loose. Justice is an harmonical thing. Herbs hot or cold beyond a certain degree, kill. We see even contrary elements preserved in one body by a wise contemperation. Justice in rigour is oft extreme injustice, where some considerable circumstances should incline to moderation; and the reckoning will be easier for bending rather to moderation than rigour.

Insolent carriage toward miserable persons, if humbled, is unseemly in any who look for mercy themselves. Misery should be a loadstone of mercy, not a footstool for pride to trample on.

Sometimes it falleth out that those that are under the government of others, are most injurious by waywardness and harsh censures, herein disparaging and discouraging the endeavours of superiors for public good. In so great weakness of man's nature, and especially in this crazy age of the world, we ought to take in good part any moderate happiness we enjoy by government; and not be altogether as a nail in the wound, exasperating things by misconstruction. Here love should have a mantle to cast upon lesser errors of those above us. Oftentimes the poor man is the oppressor by unjust clamours. We should labour to give the best interpretation to the actions of governors that the nature of the actions will possibly bear.

In the last place, there is something for private Christians, even for all of us in our common relations, to take notice of: we are debtors to the weak in many things.

1. Let us be watchful in the use of our liberty, and labour to be inoffensive in our carriage, that our example compel them not. There is a commanding force in an example, as Peter, Gal. ii. Looseness of life is cruelty to ourselves, and to the souls of others. Though we cannot keep them from perishing which will perish, in regard of the event; yet if we do that which is apt of itself to destroy the souls of others, their ruin is imputable to us.

2. Let men take heed of taking up Satan's office, in depraving the good actions of others, as

he did Job's, "doth he serve God for nought?" Job i. 9, or slandering their persons, judging of them according to the wickedness that is in their own hearts. The devil getteth more by such discouragements, and these reproaches that are cast upon religion, than by fire and faggot. These, as unseasonable frosts, nip all gracious offers in the bud; and as much as in them lieth, with Herod, labour to kill Christ in young professors. A Christian is a hallowed and a sacred thing, Christ's temple; "and he that destroyeth his temple, him will Christ destroy," 1 Cor. iii. 17.

3. Amongst the things that are to be taken heed of, there is amongst private Christians a bold usurpation of censure towards others, not considering their temptations. Some will unchurch and unbrother in a passion. But distempers do not alter true relations; though the child in a fit should disclaim the mother, yet the mother will not disclaim the child.

There is therefore in these judging times good ground of St. James' caveat, that there should not "be too many masters," James iii. 1; that we should not smite one another by hasty censures, especially in things of an indifferent nature; some things are as the mind of him is that doth them, or doth them not; for both may be unto the Lord.

A holy aim in things of a middle nature makes the judgments of men, although seemingly contrary, yet not so much blameable. Christ, for the good aims he seeth in us, overlooketh any ill in them, so far as not to lay it to our charge.

Men must not be too curious in prying into the weaknesses of others. We should labour rather to see what they have that is for eternity, to incline our heart to love them, than into that weakness which the Spirit of God will in time consume, to estrange us. Some think it strength of grace to endure nothing in the weaker, whereas the strongest are readiest to bear with the infirmities of the weak.

Where most holiness is, there is most moderation, where it may be without prejudice of piety to God and the good of others. We see in Christ a marvellous temper of absolute holiness, with great moderation, in this text. What had become of our salvation if he had stood upon terms, and not stooped thus low unto us? We need not affect to be more holy than Christ; it is no flattery to do as he doth, so it be to edification.

The Holy Ghost is content to dwell in smoky, offensive souls. O, that that Spirit would breathe into our spirits the like merciful disposition!

We endure the bitterness of wormwood, and other distasteful plants and herbs, only because we have some experience of some wholesome quality in them ; and why should we reject men of useful parts and graces, only for some harshness of disposition, which, as it is offensive to us, so grieveth themselves ?

Grace whilst we live here is in souls, which as they are imperfectly renewed, so they dwell in bodies subject to several humours, which will incline the soul sometimes to excess in one passion, sometimes to excess in another.

Bucer was a deep and a moderate divine ; upon long experience he resolved to refuse none in whom he saw, *aliquid Christi*, something of Christ.

The best Christians in this state of imperfection are like gold that is a little too light, which needs some grains of allowance to make it pass. You must grant the best their allowance. We must supply out of our love and mercy, that which we see wanting in them.

The church of Christ is a common hospital, wherein all are in some measure sick of some spiritual disease or other ; that we should all have ground of exercising mutually the spirit of wisdom and meekness.

1. This that we may the better do, let us put upon ourselves the Spirit of Christ. The Spirit of God carrieth a majesty with it. Corruption will hardly yield to corruption in another. Pride is intolerable to pride. The weapons of this warfare must not be carnal, 2 Cor. x. 4. The great apostles would not set upon the work of the ministry, until they were " clothed as it were with power from on high," Luke xxiv. 49. The Spirit will only work with his own tools. And we should think what affection Christ would carry to the party in this case. That great physician, as he had a quick eye and a healing tongue, so had he a gentle hand, and a tender heart.

2. And secondly, put upon us the condition of him whom we deal withal : we are, or have been, or may be such : make the case our own, and withal consider in what near relation a Christian standeth unto us, even as a brother, a fellow-member, heir of the same salvation. And therefore let us take upon ourselves a tender care of them every way ; and especially in cherishing the peace of their consciences. Conscience is a tender and delicate thing, and so must be used. It is like a lock, if the wards be troubled, it will be troublesome to open.

CHAP. X.—*Rules to try whether we be such as Christ will not quench.*

For trial, to let us see whether we be this smoking flax which Christ will not quench. In this trial remember these :—1. *Rules.* 2. *Signs.*

1. We must have two eyes, one to see imperfections in ourselves and others ; the other to see what is good. "I am black," saith the church, "but yet comely," Cant. i. 5. Those ever want comfort that are much in quarrelling with themselves, and through their infirmities are prone to feed upon such bitter things, as will most nourish that distemper they are sick of. These delight to be looking on the dark side of the cloud only.

2. We must not judge of ourselves always according to present feeling ; for in temptations we shall see nothing but smoke of distrustful thoughts. Fire may be raked up in the ashes, though not seen ; life in the winter is hid in the root.

3. Take heed of false reasoning ; as because our fire doth not blaze out as others, therefore we have no fire at all ; and by false conclusions come to sin against the commandment in bearing false witness against ourselves. The prodigal

would not say he was no son, but that he was not worthy to be called a son, Luke xv. 19. We must neither trust to false evidence, nor deny true; for so we should dishonour the work of God's spirit in us, and lose the help of that evidence which would cherish our love to Christ, and arm us against Satan's discouragements. Some are so faulty this way, as if they had been hired by Satan, the "accuser of the brethren," Rev. xii. 10, to plead for him, in accusing themselves.

4. Know, for a ground of this, that in the covenant of grace, God requires the truth of grace, not any certain measure; and a spark of fire is fire as well as the whole element. Therefore we must look to grace in the spark as well as in the flame. All have not the like strong, yet the like precious faith, 2 Pet. i. 1, whereby they lay hold, and put on, the perfect righteousness of Christ. A weak hand may receive a rich jewel; a few grapes will show that the plant is a vine, and not a thorn. It is one thing to be wanting in grace, and another thing to want grace altogether. God knoweth we have nothing of ourselves, therefore in the covenant of grace he requireth no more than he giveth, and giveth what he requireth, and accepteth what he giveth:

"He that hath not a lamb may bring a pair of turtle doves," Lev. xii. 6. What is the Gospel itself but a merciful moderation, in which Christ's obedience is esteemed ours, and our sins laid upon him, and wherein God of a judge becometh the father, pardoning our sins and accepting our obedience, though feeble and blemished! We are now brought to heaven under the covenant of grace by a way of love and mercy.

It will prove a special help to know distinctly the difference between the covenant of works and the covenant of grace, between Moses and Christ; Moses without all mercy breaketh all bruised reeds, and quencheth all smoking flax. For the law requireth, 1, personal; 2, perpetual; 3, perfect obedience; 4, and from a perfect heart; and that under a most terrible curse, and giveth no strength, a severe taskmaster, like Pharaoh's requiring the whole tale, and yet giving no straw. Christ cometh with blessing after blessing even upon those whom Moses had cursed, and with healing balm for those wounds which Moses had made.

The same duties are required in both covenants; as "to love the Lord with all our hearts, with all our souls," etc., Deut. vi. 5. In the covenant of works, this must be taken in the rigour; but under the covenant of grace, as it is a sincere endeavour proportionable to grace received (and so it must be understood of Josias, and others, when it is said, "they loved God with all their hearts," etc.), it must have an evangelical mitigation.

The law is sweetened by the Gospel, and becometh delightful to the inner man, Rom. vii. 22. Under this gracious covenant sincerity is perfection. This is the death in the pot in the Roman religion, that they confound two covenants; and it deads the comfort of drooping ones, that they cannot distinguish them. And thus they suffer themselves to be "held under bondage," Isa. lxi. 1, 2, when Christ hath set them free; and stay themselves in the prison, when Christ hath set open the doors before them.

5. Grace sometimes is so little as is undiscernible to us; the Spirit sometimes hath secret operations in us, which we know not for the present; but Christ knoweth. Sometimes in bitterness of temptation, when the Spirit struggles with sense of God's anger, we are apt to think God an enemy; and a troubled soul is like troubled water, we can see nothing in it; and so far as it is not cleansed, it will cast up mire and dirt. It is full of objections against itself, yet for

the most part we may discern something of the hidden life, and of these smothered sparks.

In a gloomy day there is so much light whereby we may know it to be day, and not night; so there is something in a Christian under a cloud, whereby he may be discerned to be a true believer, and not a hypocrite. There is no mere darkness in the state of grace, but some beam of light, whereby the kingdom of darkness wholly prevaileth not.

CHAP. XI.—*Signs of smoking flax which Christ will not quench.*

These things premised, let us know for a trial, 1. First, *if there be any holy fire in us, it is kindled from heaven* by the "Father of lights, who commandeth light to shine out of darkness," 2 Cor. iv. 6. As it is kindled in the use of means, so it is fed. The light in us, and the light in the Word, spring one from the other, and both from one Holy Spirit; and, therefore, those that regard not the Word, it is because there "is no light in them," Isa. viii. 20. Heavenly truths must have a heavenly light to discern them. Natural men see heavenly things, but not in their own proper light, but by an inferior light. God in every converted man putteth a light into the eye of his soul, proportionable to the light of truths revealed unto him. A carnal eye will never see spiritual things.

2. Secondly, *the least divine light hath heat with it in some measure;* light in the understanding breedeth heat of love in the affections. *Claritas in intellectu parit ardorem in affectu.* In what measure the sanctified understanding seeth a thing to be true, or good, in that measure the will embraces it. Weak light breeds weak inclinations; a strong light, strong inclinations. A little spiritual light is of strength enough to answer strong objections of flesh and blood, and to look through all earthly allurements and opposing hindrances, presenting them as far inferior to those heavenly objects it eyeth.

All light that is not spiritual, because it wanteth the strength of sanctifying grace, yieldeth to every little temptation, especially when it is fitted and suited to personal inclinations. This is the reason why Christians that have light, little for quantity, but yet heavenly for quality, hold out, when men of larger apprehensions sink.

This prevailing of light in the soul is because, together with the spirit of illumination, there goeth, in the godly, a spirit of power, 2 Tim. i. 7, to subdue the heart to truth revealed, and to put a taste and relish into the will, suitable to the sweetness of the truths; else a mere natural will will rise against supernatural truths, as having an antipathy and enmity against them. In the godly, holy truths are conveyed by way of a taste; gracious men have a spiritual palate as well as a spiritual eye. Grace altereth the relish.

3. Thirdly, where this heavenly light is kindled *it directeth in the right way.* For it is given for that use, to shew us the best way, and to guide in the particular passages of life; if otherwise, it is but common light, given only for the good of others. Some have light of knowledge, yet follow not that light, but are guided by carnal reason and policy; such as the prophet speaks of, "All you that kindle a fire, walk in the light of your own fire, and in the sparks that you have kindled; but this you shall have of mine hand, ye shall lie down in sorrow," Isa. l. 11. God delights to confound carnal wisdom, as enmity to him, and robbing him of his prerogative, who is God only wise. We must, therefore, walk by his light, and not the blaze of our own fire. God must light our candle, Ps. xviii. 28, or else we are like to abide in darkness. Those sparks

that are not kindled from heaven, are not strong enough to keep us from lying down in sorrow, though they make a greater blaze and show than the light from above, as madmen do greater things than sober, but by a false strength : so the excess of these men's joy ariseth from a false light, "the candle of the wicked shall be put out," Job xviii. 6.

The light that some men have, it is like light-ning, which after a sudden flash leaveth them more in darkness. They can love the light as it shines, but hate it as it discovers and directs. A little holy light will enable to keep the word, and not betray religion, and deny Christ's name, as Christ speaketh of the church of Philadelphia, Rev. iii. 8.

4. Fourthly, where this fire is, *it will sever things of diverse natures, and shew a difference between things, as gold and dross.* It will sever between flesh and spirit, and shew that this is of nature, this of grace. All is not ill in a bad action, or good in a good action. There is gold in ore, which God and his Spirit in us can distin-guish. A carnal man's heart is like a dungeon, wherein is nothing to be seen but horror and confusion ; this light maketh us judicious and humble, upon clearer sight of God's purity, and

our own uncleanness; and maketh us able to discern of the work of the Spirit in another.

5. Fifthly, so far as a man is spiritual, *so far is light delightful unto him*, as willing to see anything amiss, that he may reform, and any further service discovered that he may perform, because he truly hateth ill and loveth good; if he goeth against light discovered, he will soon be reclaimed, because light hath a friendly party within him. Whereupon, at a little sight of his error he is soon counselable, as David in his intendment to kill Nabal, and blessed God afterwards, when he stopped in an ill way, 1 Sam. xxv. 32.

In a carnal man, the light breaks in upon him, but he labours to shut the passages, he hath no delight to come to the light. It is impossible before the Spirit of grace hath subdued the heart, but that it should sin against the light, either by resisting of it, or keeping it prisoner under base lusts, and burying it, as it were, in the earth; or perverting of it, and so making it an agent and factor for the flesh, in searching out arguments to plead for it, or abusing that little measure of light they have, to keep out a greater, higher, and more heavenly light; and so, at length, make that light they have a misleading guide to utter darkness. And the reason is, because it hath no friend within, the soul is in a contrary frame; and light always hindereth that sinful peace that men are willing to speak to themselves: whence we see it oft enrages men the more, as the sun in the spring breedeth aguish distempers, because it stirreth humours, and doth not waste them. There is nothing in the world more unquiet than the heart of a wicked man, that sitteth under means of knowledge, until, like a thief, he hath put out the candle, that he may sin with the less check. Spiritual light is distinct, it seeth spiritual good, with application to ourselves; but common light is confused, and lets sin lie quiet. Where fire is in any degree, it will fight against the contrary matter. God hath put irreconcilable hatred between light and darkness at first, so between good and ill, flesh and spirit, Gal. v. 17; grace will never join with sin, no more than fire with water. Fire will mingle with no contrary, but preserveth its own purity, and is never corrupted as other elements are. Therefore, those that plead and plot for liberties of the flesh, shew themselves strangers from the life of God. Upon this strife, gracious men oft complain that they have no grace, but they contradict themselves in their complaints ; as if a man that seeth should complain he cannot see, or complain that he is asleep, when the very complaint, springing from a displeasure against sin, sheweth that there is something in him opposite to sin. Can a dead man complain ? Some things, though bad in themselves, yet discover good ; as smoke discovers some fire. Breaking out in the body shews strength of nature. Some infirmities discover more good than some seeming beautiful actions. Excess of passion in opposing evil, though not to be justified, yet sheweth a better spirit than a calm temper, where there is just cause of being moved. Better it is that the water should run something muddily, than not at all. Job had more grace in his distempers than his friends in their seeming wise carriage. Actions soiled with some weaknesses are more accepted than complemental performances.

6. Sixthly, fire, where it is in the least measure *is in some degree active ;* so the least measure of grace is *working*, as springing from the Spirit of God, which, from the working nature of it, is compared to fire. Nay, in sins, when there seemeth nothing active, but corruption, yet there is a contrary principle, which breaks the force of

sin, so that it is not out of measure sinful, as in those that are carnal, Rom. vii. 13.

7. Seventhly, fire maketh metals *pliable and malleable, so doth grace, where it is begun;* it worketh the heart to be pliable and ready for all good impressions.   Untractable spirits shew that they are not so much as smoking flax.

8. Eighthly, fire turneth all, as much as it can, to fire; so grace *laboureth to breed the like impression in others, and make as many good as it can.*   Grace likewise maketh a gracious use even of natural and civil things, and doth spiritualise them.   What another man doth only civilly, a gracious man will do holily.   Whether he eateth or drinketh, or whatsoever he doth, he doth all to the glory of God, 1 Cor. x. 31, making everything serviceable to the last end.

9. Ninthly, *sparks by nature fly upwards; so the Spirit of grace carrieth the soul heavenward, and setteth before us holy and heavenly aims.*   As it was kindled from heaven, so it carries us back to heaven.   The part followeth the whole: fire mounteth upward, so every spark to its own element.   Where the aim and bent of the soul is Godwards, there is grace, though opposed.   The least measure of it is holy desires springing from faith and love, for we cannot desire anything

which we do not believe first to be, and the desire of it issues from love. Hence desires are counted a part of the thing desired in some measure; but then they must be, *first, constant,* for constancy shews that they are supernaturally natural, and not enforced; *secondly*, they must be *carried to spiritual things*, as to believe, to love God, etc.: not out of a special exigent, because, if now they had grace, they think they might escape some danger, but as a loving heart is carried to the thing loved for some excellency in itself; and *thirdly*, with desire there is grief when it is hindered, which stirs up to prayer: "Oh, that my ways were so directed, that I might keep thy statutes!" Ps. cxix. 5 ; O miserable man that I am, who shall deliver ? etc., Rom. vii. 24 ; *fourthly*, desires put us onward still: Oh, that I might serve God with more liberty; Oh, that I were more free from these offensive, unsavoury, noisome lusts !

10. Tenthly, fire worketh itself, if it hath any matter to feed on, *into a larger compass, and mounteth higher and higher, and the higher it riseth, the purer is the flame;* so where true grace is, it groweth in measure and purity. Smoking flax will grow to a flame; and as it increaseth, so it worketh out the contrary, and

refineth itself more and more. *Ignis, quo magis lucet, eo minus fumat.* Therefore, it argueth a false heart to set ourselves a measure in grace, and to rest in beginnings, alleging that Christ will not quench the smoking flax. But this merciful disposition in Christ is joined with perfect holiness, shewed in perfect hatred to sin ; for rather than sin should not have its deserved punishment, himself became a sacrifice for sin, wherein his Father's holiness and his own most of all shined. And, besides this, in the work of sanctification, though he favours his work in us, yet favours he not sin in us ; for he will never take his hand from his work, until he hath taken away sin, even in its very being, from our natures. The same spirit that purified that blessed mass whereof he was made, cleanseth us by degrees to be suitable to so holy a head, and frameth the judgment and affection of all to whom he sheweth mercy, to concur with his own, in labouring to further his ends, in abolishing of sin out of our nature.

Chap. XII.—*Scruples hindering comfort removed.*

Use. From the meditation of these rules and signs, much comfort may be brought into the souls of the weakest; which, that it may be in the more abundance, let me add something for the helping them over some few ordinary objections and secret thoughts against themselves, which, getting within the heart, oftentimes keep them under.

1. Some think they have no faith at all, because they have no full assurance; whenas the fairest fire that can be will have some smoke. The best actions will smell of the smoke. The mortar wherein garlic hath been stamped will always smell of it; so all our actions will savour something of the old man.

2. In weakness of body some think grace dieth, because their performances are feeble, their spirits, being the instruments of their souls' actions, being wasted; not considering that God regards those hidden sighs of those that want abilities to express them outwardly. He that pronounceth them blessed that consider the poor, will have a merciful consideration of such himself.

3. Some again are haunted with hideous representations to their fantasies, and with vile and unworthy thoughts of God, of Christ, of the Word, etc., which, as busy flies, disquiet and molest their peace; these are cast in like wildfire by Satan, as may be discerned by the (1) strange-

ness, (2) strength and violence, (3) horribleness
of them even unto nature corrupt. *Vellum
servari Domine, sed cogitationes non patiuntur.*
A pious soul is no more guilty of them, than
Benjamin of Joseph's cup put into his sack.
Amongst other helps prescribed by godly writers,
as abomination of them, and diversion from them
to other things, etc., let this be one, to complain
unto Christ against them, and to fly under the
wings of his protection, and to desire him to take
our part against his and our enemy.   Shall every
sin and blasphemy of man be forgiven, and not
these blasphemous thoughts, which have the
devil for their father, when Christ himself was
therefore molested in this kind, that he might
succour all poor souls in the like case?

But there is a difference betwixt Christ and us
in this case, by reason that Satan had nothing of
his own in Christ, his suggestions left no
impression at all in his holy nature; but, as
sparks falling into the sea, were presently
quenched. Satan's temptations of Christ were
only suggestions on Satan's part, and apprehensions of the vileness of them on Christ's part,
To apprehend ill suggested by another, is not ill.
It was Christ's grievance, but Satan's sin. But
thus he yielded himself to be tempted, that he

might both pity us in our conflicts, and train us up to manage our spiritual weapons as he did. Christ could have overcome him by power, but he did it by argument. But when Satan cometh to us, he findeth something of his own in us, which holdeth correspondency and hath intelligence with him ; there is the same enmity in our nature to God and goodness in some degree, that is in Satan himself; whereupon his temptations fasten for the most part some taint upon us. And if there wanted a devil to suggest, yet sinful thoughts would arise from within us ; though none were cast in from without, we have a mint of them within : these thoughts, *morosa cogitatio*, if the soul dwell on them so long as to suck or draw from and by them any sinful delight, then they leave a more heavy guilt upon the soul, and hinder our sweet communion with God, and interrupt our peace, and put a contrary relish into the soul, disposing of it to greater sins. All scandalous breakings out are but thoughts at the first. Ill thoughts are as little thieves, which, creeping in at the window, open the door to greater ; thoughts are seeds of actions. These, especially when they are helped forward by Satan, make the life of many good Christians almost a martyrdom. In this case it

is an unsound comfort that some minister, that
ill thoughts arise from nature, and what is
natural is excusable; but we must know, that
nature, as it came out of God's hands at the first,
had no such risings out of it: the soul, as
inspired of God, had no such unsavoury breath-
ings; but since that by sin it betrayed itself, it
is in some sort natural to it to forge sinful
imaginations, and to be a furnace of such sparks;
and this is an aggravation of the sinfulness of
natural corruption, that it is so deeply rooted,
and so generally spread in our nature.

It furthereth humiliation to know the whole
breadth and depth of sin; only this, that our
nature now, so far as it is unrenewed, is so
unhappily fruitful in ill thoughts, ministers this
comfort, that it is not our case alone, as if our
condition herein were severed from others, as
some have been tempted to think, even almost to
despair; none, say they, have such a loathsome
nature as I have. This springs from ignorance
of the spreading of original sin, for what can
come from an unclean thing, but that which is
unclean? "As in the water face answers face, so
the polluted heart of one man answereth to the
heart of another," Prov. xxvii. 19, where grace
hath not made some difference. As in annoy-

ances from Satan, so here, the best way is to lay open our complaints to Christ, and cry with St. Paul, *Domine sim patior*, "O miserable man that I am, who shall deliver me from this body of death?" Rom. vii. 24, 25 : upon this venting of his distressed soul, he presently found comfort ; for he breaketh into thanksgiving, "Thanks be to God," etc. And it is good to take advantage from hence to hate this noisome body of death the more, and to draw nearer unto God, as that holy man after his "foolish and beastly thoughts," Ps. lxxiii. 22 and 28, did, and to keep our hearts closer to God, seasoning them with heavenly meditations in the morning, storing up good matter that our heart may be a good treasury, and begging of Christ his Holy Spirit to stop that cursed issue, and to be a living spring of better thoughts in us. Nothing more abaseth the spirits of holy men that desire to delight in God after they have escaped the common defilements of the world, than these unclean issues of spirit, as being most contrary to God, who is a pure Spirit : but the very irksomeness of them yields matter of comfort against them ; they force the soul to all spiritual exercises, to watchfulness, and a more near walking with God, and to raise itself to thoughts of a higher nature, which the truth of God, works of God, communion of saints, the mystery of godliness, the consideration of the terror of the Lord, of the excellency of the state of a Christian, and conversation suitable, do abundantly minister. They discover to us a necessity of daily purging and pardoning grace, and of seeking to be found in Christ, and so bring the best often upon their knees.

But our chief comfort is, that our blessed Saviour, as he bade Satan avaunt from himself after he had given way awhile to his impudency, Matt. iv. 10 ; so he will command him to be gone from us, when it shall be good for us ; he must be gone at a word. And he can and will likewise in his due time rebuke the rebellious and extravagant stirrings of our hearts, and bring all the thoughts of the inner man in subjection to himself.

4. Some think, when they begin once to be troubled with the smoke of corruption more than they were before, therefore they are worse than they were. It is true, that corruptions appear now more than before, but they are less.

For, first, sin, the more it is seen the more it is hated, and thereupon is the less. Motes are in a room before the sun shines, but they then only appear.

Secondly, contraries, the nearer they are one to another, the sharper is the conflict betwixt them : now of all enemies the spirit and the flesh are nearest one to another, being both in the soul of a regenerate man, and in faculties of the soul, and in every action that springeth from those faculties, and therefore it is no marvel the soul, the seat of this battle, thus divided in itself, be as smoking flax.

Thirdly, the more grace, the more spiritual life, and the more spiritual life, the more antipathy to the contrary; when none are so sensible of corruption, as those that have the most living souls.

And fourthly, when men give themselves to carnal liberties, their corruptions trouble them not, as not being bound and tied up ; but when once grace suppresseth their extravagant and licentious excesses, then the flesh boileth, as disdaining to be confined ; yet they are better now than they were before. That matter which yields smoke was in the torch before it was lighted ; but it is not offensive till the torch begins to burn. Let such know, that if the smoke be once offensive to them, it is a sign that there is light. It is better to enjoy the benefit of light, though with smoke, than to be altogether in the dark.

Neither is smoke so offensive, as light is comfortable to us, it yielding an evidence of truth of grace in the heart; therefore, though it be cumbersome in the conflict, yet it is comfortable in the evidence. It is better corruption should offend us now, than by giving way to it to redeem a little peace with loss of comfort afterwards. Let such, therefore, as are at variance and odds with their corruptions, look upon this text as their portion of comfort.

Chap. XIII.—*Set upon Duties notwithstanding Weaknesses.*

Here is a use of encouragement to duty, that Christ will not quench the smoking flax, but blow it up. Some are loth to perform good duties, because they feel their hearts rebelling, and duties come off untowardly. We should not avoid good actions for the infirmities cleaving unto them. Christ looketh more at the good in them that he meaneth to cherish, than the ill in them that he meaneth to abolish. A sick man, though in eating he something increaseth the disease, yet he will eat, that nature may get strength against the disease; so though sin cleaveth to what we do, yet let us do it, since we have to deal with so good a Lord, and the more strife we meet withal, the more acceptance. Christ loveth to taste of the good fruits that come from us, although they will always relish of the old stock. A Christian complaineth he cannot pray. Oh, I am troubled with so many distracting thoughts, and never more than now. But hath he put into thine heart a desire to pray? He will hear the desires of his own Spirit in thee. "We know not what to pray for as we ought" (nor do anything else as we ought), "but the Spirit helpeth our infirmities, with inexpressible sighs and groans," Rom. viii. 26, which are not hid from God. "My groanings are not hid from thee," Ps. xxxviii. 9. God can pick sense out of a confused prayer. These desires cry louder in his ears than thy sins. Sometimes a Christian hath such confused thoughts, he can say nothing, but as a child crieth, O Father, not able to shew what it needs, as Moses at the Red Sea.

These stirrings of spirit touch the bowels of God, and melt him into compassion towards us, when they come from the spirit of adoption, and from a striving to be better.

Object. Oh, but is it possible, thinketh the misgiving heart, that so holy a God should accept such a prayer?

Ans. Yes, he will accept that which is his own, and pardon that which is ours. "Jonah prayed in the whale's belly," Jonah ii. 1, being burdened with the guilt of sin, yet God heareth him. Let not, therefore, infirmities discourage us. St. James takes away this objection, v. 17. Some might object, If I were as holy as Elias, then my prayers might be regarded; but, saith he, "Elias was a man of like passions to us," he had his passions as well as we; for do we think that God heard him because he was without fault? No, surely. But look we to the promises.: "Call upon me in the day of trouble, and I will hear thee," Ps. l. 15; "Ask and ye shall receive," Matt. vii, 7; and such like. God accepteth our prayers, though weak. 1. Because we are his own children, they come from his own Spirit. 2. Because they are according to his own will. 3. Because they are offered in Christ's mediation, and he takes them, and mingleth them with his own odours, Rev. viii. 3. There is never a holy sigh, never a tear we shed, lost. And as every grace increaseth by exercise of itself, so doth the grace of prayer. By prayer we learn to pray. So, likewise, we should take heed of a spirit of discouragement in all other holy duties, since we have so gracious a Saviour. Pray as we are able, hear as we are able, strive as we are able, do as we are able, according to the measure of grace received. God in Christ will cast a gracious eye upon that which is his own. Would St. Paul do nothing, because "he could not do the good he would?" Phil. iii. 14. Yes, he "pressed to the mark." Let us not be cruel to ourselves when Christ is thus gracious.

There is a certain meekness of spirit whereby we yield thanks to God for any ability at all, and rest quiet with the measure of grace received, seeing it is God's good pleasure it should be so, who giveth the will and the deed, yet so as we rest not from further endeavours. But when, upon faithful endeavour, we come short of that we would be, and short of that others are, then know for our comfort, Christ will not quench the smoking flax, and that sincerity and truth, as before was said, with endeavour of growth, is our perfection. It is comfortable what God saith, "He only shall go to his grave in peace, because there is some goodness," 1 Kings xiv. 13; though but some goodness. "Lord, I believe," Mark ix. 24, with a weak faith, yet with faith; love thee with a faint love, yet with love; endeavour in a feeble manner, yet endeavour. A little fire is fire, though it smoketh. Since thou hast taken

me into thy covenant to be thine of an enemy,
wilt thou cast me off for these infirmities, which,
as they displease thee, so are they the grief of my
own heart?

CHAP. XIV.—*The case of Indisposition resolved, and
Discouragements.*

1. From what hath been spoken, with some
little addition, it will not be difficult to resolve
that case which some require help in, namely,
whether we ought to perform duties, our hearts
being altogether indisposed. For satisfaction we
must know, 1. Our hearts of themselves do linger
after liberty, and are hardly brought under the
yoke of duty; and the more spiritual the duty
is, the more is their untowardness. Corruption
getteth ground, for the most part, in every
neglect. It is as in rowing against the tide, one
stroke neglected will not be gained in three; and
therefore it is good to keep our hearts close to
duty, and not to hearken unto the excuses they
are ready to frame.

2. In the setting upon duty, God strengtheneth
his own party that he hath in us. We find a
warmness of heart, and increase of strength, the
Spirit going along with us, and raising us up by

degrees, until it leaveth us as it were in heaven. God often delighteth to take the advantage of our indisposition, that he may manifest his work the more clearly, and that all the glory of the work may be his, whose all the strength is.

3. Obedience is most direct when there is nothing else to sweeten the action. Although the sacrifice be imperfect, yet the obedience with which it is offered hath acceptance.

4. That which is won as a spoil from our corruptions will have such a degree of comfort afterwards, as for the present it hath of cumber. Feeling and freeness of spirit is oft reserved until duty be discharged; reward followeth work. In and after duty we find that experience of God's presence which, without obedience, we may long wait for, and yet go without. This hindereth not the Spirit's freedom in blowing upon our souls when it listeth, John iii. 8. For we speak only of such a state of soul as is becalmed, and must row, as it were, against the stream. As in sailing, the hand must be to the stern, and the eye to the star ; so here, put forth that little strength we have to duty, and look up for assistance, which the Spirit, as freely, so seasonably will afford.

Caution. (1.) Yet in these duties, that require

as well the body as the soul, there may be a cessation till strength be repaired. Whetting doth not let, but fit. (2.) In sudden passions there should be a time to compose and calm the soul, and to put the strings in tune. The prophet would have a minstrel to bring his soul into frame, 1 Sam. xvi. 16, 17.

So likewise we are subject to discouragements in suffering, by reason of impatiency in us. Alas! I shall never get through such a cross. But if God bring us into the cross, he will be with us in the cross, and at length bring us out more refined; we shall lose nothing but dross, Zech. xiii. 9. Of our own strength we cannot bear the least trouble, and by the Spirit's assistance we can bear the greatest. The Spirit will join his shoulders to help us to bear our infirmities. "The Lord will put his hand to heave us up," Ps. xxxvii. 24. "You have heard of the patience of Job," saith James, chap. v. 11. We have heard likewise of his impatiency too; but it pleased God mercifully to overlook that. It yields us comfort also in desolate conditions, as contagious sicknesses, and the like, wherein we are more immediately under God's hand. Then Christ hath a throne of mercy at our bed's side, and numbers our tears and our groans. And, to come to the matter we are now about, the Sacrament,* it was ordained not for angels, but for men ; and not for perfect men, but for weak men ; and not for Christ, who is truth itself, to bind him, but because we are ready, by reason of our guilty and unbelieving hearts, to call truth itself into question. Therefore it was not enough for his goodness to leave us many precious promises, but he giveth us seals to strengthen us : and, what though we are not so prepared as we should, yet let us pray as Hezekiah did : "The Lord pardon every one that prepareth his heart to seek the Lord God of his fathers, though he be not cleansed according to the purification of the sanctuary," 2 Chron. xxx. 19. Then we come comfortably to this holy sacrament, and with much fruit. This should carry us through all duties with much cheerfulness, that, if we hate our corruptions, and strive against them, they shall not be counted ours. It is not I, saith St. Paul, but "sin that dwelleth in me," Rom. vii. 17 ; for what displeaseth us shall never hurt us, *quod non placet, non nocet,* and we shall be esteemed of God to be that we love, and desire, and labour to be. What we

---

* This was preached at the Sacrament.

desire to be we shall be, and what we desire truly to conquer we shall conquer ; for God will fulfil the desire of them that fear him, Ps. cxlv. 19. The desire is an earnest of the thing desired. How little encouragement will carry us to the affairs of this life ! And yet all the helps God offers will hardly prevail with our backward natures. Whence are, then, discouragements ?

1. Not from the Father, for he hath bound himself in covenant " to pity us as a father pitieth his children," Ps. ciii. 13, and to accept as a father our weak endeavours ; and what is wanting in the strength of duty, he giveth us leave to take up in his gracious indulgence, whereby we shall honour that grace wherein he delights, as much as in more perfect performances. *Possibilitas tua mensura tua.*

2. Not from Christ, for he by office will not quench the smoking flax. We see how Christ bestoweth the best fruits of his love upon persons, for condition mean, for parts weak, for infirmities, nay, for grosser falls, offensive : *First*, thus it pleaseth him to confound the pride of flesh, which usually taketh measure of God's love by some outward excellency. *Secondly*, thus he is delighted to shew the freedom of his grace and his prerogative royal, that " whoso-

ever glorieth, may glory in the Lord," 1 Cor. i. 31.

In the eleventh to the Hebrews, among that cloud of witnesses, we see Rahab, Gideon, and Samson, ranked with Abraham, the father of the faithful, Heb. xi. 31, 32. Our blessed Saviour, as he was the image of his Father, so in this he was of the same mind, glorifying his Father for revealing the mystery of the Gospel to simple men, neglecting those that carried the chief reputation of wisdom in the world, Heb. xi. 31, 32.

It is not unworthy of the remembering that which St. Augustine speaketh of a silly man in his time, destitute almost altogether of the use of reason, who when he was most patient of all injuries done to himself, yet, from a reverence of religion, he would not endure any injury done to the name of Christ; insomuch that he would cast stones at those that blasphemed, and would not in that case spare his own governors; which sheweth that the parts of none are so low, as that they are beneath the gracious regard of Christ; where it pleaseth him to make his choice, and to exalt his mercy, he passeth by no degree of wit, though never so plain.

3. Neither do discouragements come from the Spirit; he helps our infirmities, and by office is a

Comforter, Rom. viii. 26. If he convinceth of sin, and so humbleth us, it is that he may make way to shew his office of comforting us. Discouragements, then, must come from ourselves and Satan, who laboureth to fasten on us a loathing of duty.

Chap. XV.—*Of Infirmities. No cause of Discouragement. In whom they are. And how to recover Peace lost.*

And among other causes of discouragement, some are much vexed with scruples, even against the best duties; partly by distemper of body, helped by Satan's malice, casting dust in their eyes, in their way to heaven; and partly from some remainder of ignorance, which like darkness breedeth fears; and as ignorance of other things, so especially of this merciful disposition in Christ, the persuasion of which would easily banish false fears, they conceive of him as one sitting at a catch for all advantages against them; wherein they may see how they wrong not only themselves but his goodness. This scrupulosity, for the most part, is a sign of a godly soul, as some weeds are of a good soil: therefore are they the more to be pitied, for it is a heavy affliction, and the ground of it in most is not so much from trouble of conscience, as from sickness of fantasy. The end of Christ's coming was to free us from all such groundless fears.

There is still in some, such ignorance of that comfortable condition we are in under the covenant of grace, as by it they are much discouraged. Therefore we must know, 1. That weaknesses do not break covenant with God. They do not between husband and wife; and shall we make ourselves more pitiful than Christ, who maketh himself a pattern of love to all other husbands?

2. Weaknesses do not debar us from mercy, nay, they incline God the more, Ps. lxxviii. 39. Mercy is a part of the church's jointure, "Christ marries her in mercy," Hos. ii. 19. The husband is bound to bear with the wife, as "being the weaker vessel," 1 Pet. iii. 7; and shall we think he will exempt himself from his own rule, and not bear with his weak spouse?

3. If Christ should not be merciful to our infirmities, he should not have a people to serve him.

Put case therefore, we be very weak, yet so long as we are not found amongst malicious opposers and underminers of God's truth, let us not give way to despairing thoughts; we have a merciful Saviour. But lest we flatter ourselves without ground, we must know that weaknesses are accounted either, 1, Imperfections cleaving to our best actions ; or, 2, Such actions as proceed from want of age in Christ, whilst we are babes ; or, 3, From want of strength, where there hath been little means ; or, 4, They are sudden indeliberate breakings out, contrary to our general bent and purpose, whilst our judgment is overcast with the cloud of a sudden temptation. After which, 1, We are sensible of our infirmity ; 2, We grieve for it ; 3, And from grief, complain ; and 4, With complaining strive and labour to reform ; and 5, In labouring get some ground of our corruption.

Weaknesses so considered, howsoever they be matter of humiliation, and the object of our daily mortification, yet may stand with boldness with God, neither is a good work either extinguished by them, or tainted so far as to lose all acceptance with God. But to plead for an infirmity is more than an infirmity ; to allow ourselves in weaknesses is more than a weakness. The justification of evil sealeth up the lips, so that the soul cannot call God Father with that child-like liberty, or enjoy sweet communion with him, until peace be made by shaming ourselves, and renewing our faith. Those that have ever been

bruised for sin, if they fall they are soon recovered. Peter was recovered with a gracious
look of Christ; David by Abigail's words. Tell
a thief or a vagrant that he is out of the way,
he regards it not, because his aim is not to walk
in any certain way, but as it serveth his own
turn.

For the further clearing of this, we must conceive, 1. That wheresoever sins of infirmity are,
there in that person must be the life of grace
begun. There can be no weakness, where there
is no life. 2. There must be a sincere and
general bent to the best things; though for a
sudden a godly man be drawn or driven
aside in some particulars, yet by reason of that
interest the Spirit of Christ hath in him, and
because his aims are right for the main, he
will either recover of himself, or yield to the
counsel of others. 3. There must be a right
judgment allowing of the best ways, or else
the heart is rotten, and infuseth corruption into
the whole conversation, so that all their actions
become infected at the spring-head; they justify
looseness, and condemn God's ways, as too
much strictness; their principles whereby they
work are not good. 4. There must be a con-
jugal love to Christ, so as upon no terms they

will change their Lord and husband, and yield themselves absolutely over to be ruled by their own lusts, or the lusts of others.

A Christian's carriage towards Christ may in many things be very offensive, and cause some strangeness; yet he will own Christ, and Christ him; he will not resolve upon any way wherein he knows he must break with Christ.

Where the heart is thus in these respects qualified, there we must know this, that Christ counteth it his honour to pass by many infirmities; nay, in infirmities he perfecteth his strength. There be some almost invincible infirmities, as forgetfulness, heaviness of spirit, sudden passions, fears, etc., which, though natural, yet are for the most part tainted with sin; of these, if the life of Christ be in us, we are weary, and would fain shake them off, as a sick man his ague; otherwise it is not to be esteemed weakness so much as wilfulness, and the more will, the more sin; and little sins, when God shall awake the conscience, and "set them in order before us," Ps. l. 21, will prove great burdens, and not only bruise a reed, but shake a cedar. Yet God's children never sin with full will, because there is a contrary law of the mind, whereby the dominion of sin is broken, which always hath some secret working against the law of sin. Notwithstanding there may be so much will in a sinful action, as may wonderfully waste our comfort afterward, and keep us long upon the rack of a disquieted conscience, God in his fatherly dispensation suspending the sense of his love. So much as we give way to our will in sinning, in such a measure of distance we set ourselves from comfort. Sin against conscience is as a thief in the candle, which wasteth our joy, and thereby weakeneth our strength. We must know, therefore, that wilful breaches in sanctification will much hinder the sense of our justification.

Quest. What course shall such take to recover their peace?

Ans. Such must give a sharp sentence against themselves, and yet cast themselves upon God's mercy in Christ, as at their first conversion. And now they had need to clasp about Christ the faster, as they see more need in themselves, and let them remember the mildness of Christ here, that will not quench the smoking flax. Ofttimes we see that, after a deep humiliation, Christ speaks more peace than before, to witness the truth of this reconciliation, because he knows Satan's enterprises in casting down such lower,

and because such are most abased in themselves,
and are ashamed to look Christ in the face, by
reason of their unkindness. We see God did
not only pardon David, but after much bruising
gave him wise Solomon to succeed him in the
kingdom. We see in the Canticles, chap. vi. 44,
that the Church after she had been humbled for
her slighting of Christ, Christ sweetly entertains
her again, and falleth into commendation of her
beauty. We must know for our comfort that
Christ was not anointed to this great work of
the Mediator for lesser sins only, but for the
greatest, if we have but a spark of true faith to
lay hold on him. Therefore, if there be any
bruised reed, let him not except himself, when
Christ doth not except him; "Come unto me
all ye that are weary and heavy laden," etc.,
Matt. xi. 28. Why should we not make use of
so gracious a disposition ? we are only therefore
poor, because we know not our riches in Christ.
In time of temptation, rather believe Christ than
the devil, believe truth from truth itself, hearken
not to a liar, an enemy, and a murderer.

CHAP. XVI.—*Satan not to be believed, as he representeth Christ unto us.*

Since Christ is thus comfortably set out unto us, let us not believe Satan's representations of him. When we are troubled in conscience for our sins, his manner is then to present him to the afflicted soul as a most severe judge, armed with justice against us. But then let us present him to our souls, as thus offered to our view by God himself, as holding out a sceptre of mercy, and · spreading his arms to receive us. When we think of Joseph, Daniel, John the Evangelist, etc., we frame conceits of them with delight, as of mild and sweet persons ; much more when we think of Christ, we should conceive of him as a mirror of all meekness. If the sweetness of all flowers were in one, how sweet must that flower needs be ? In Christ all perfections of mercy and love meet ; how great then must that mercy be that lodgeth in so gracious a heart ? whatsoever tenderness is scattered in husband, father, brother, head, all is but a beam from him, it is in him in the most eminent manner. We are weak, but we are his ; we are deformed, but yet carry his image upon us. A father looks not so much at the blemishes of his child, as at his own nature in him ; so Christ finds matter of love from that which is his own in us. He sees his own nature in us: we are diseased, but yet his members. Who ever neglected his own members because they were sick or weak ? none ever hated his own flesh. Can the head forget the members ? can Christ forget himself? we are his fulness, as he is ours. He was love itself clothed with man's nature, which he united so near to himself, that he might communicate his goodness the more freely unto us ; and took not our nature when it was at the best, but when it was abased, with all natural and common infirmities it was subject unto. Let us therefore abhor all suspicious thoughts, as either cast in or cherished by that damned spirit, who as he laboured to divide between the Father and the Son by jealousies, " If thou be the Son of God," etc., Matt. iv. 6, so his daily study is, to divide betwixt the Son and us, by breeding mispersuasions in us of Christ, as if there were not such tender love in him to such as we are. It was his art from the beginning to discredit God with man, by calling God's love into question, with our first father Adam ; his success then makes him ready at that weapon still.

Object. But for all this, I feel not Christ so to me, saith the smoking flax, but rather the clean contrary; he seemeth to be an enemy unto me, I see and feel evidences of his just displeasure.

Ans. Christ may act the part of an enemy a little while, as Joseph did, but it is to make way for acting his own part of mercy in a more seasonable time; he cannot hold in his bowels long. He seemeth to wrestle with us, as with Jacob, but he supplies us with hidden strength, at length to get the better. Faith pulls off the vizard from his face, and sees a loving heart under contrary appearances. *Fiddes Christo larvam detrahit.* At first he answers the woman of Canaan crying after him not a word; 2, Then gives her a denial; 3, Gives an answer tending to her reproach, calling her dog, as being without the covenant; yet she would not be so beaten off, for she considered the end of his coming. As his father was never nearer him in strength to support him, than when he was furthest off in sense of favour to comfort him; so Christ is never nearer us in power to uphold us, than when he seemeth most to hide his presence from us. The influence of the Sun of Righteousness pierceth deeper than his light. In such cases, whatsoever Christ's present carriage is towards us, let us oppose his nature and office against it ; he cannot deny himself, he cannot but discharge the office his Father hath laid upon him.   We see here the Father hath undertaken that he shall not "quench the smoking flax ;" and Christ again undertaking for us to the Father, appearing before him for us, until he presents us blameless before him, John xvii. 6, 11.   The Father hath given us to Christ, and Christ giveth us back again to the Father.

Object. This were good comfort, if I were but as smoking flax.

Ans. It is well that thy objection pincheth upon thyself, and not upon Christ ; it is well thou givest him the honour of his mercy towards others, though not to thyself: but yet do not wrong the work of his Spirit in thy heart.   Satan, as he slandereth Christ to us, so he slandereth us to ourselves.   If thou be not so much as smoking flax, then why dost thou not renounce thy interest in Christ, and disclaim the covenant of grace ?   This thou darest not do.   Why dost thou not give up thyself wholly to other contents ?   This thy spirit will not suffer thee. Whence come these restless groanings and complaints ? lay this thy present estate, together with this office of Christ to such, and do not despise the consolation of the Almighty, nor refuse thy own mercy. Cast thyself into the arms of Christ, and if thou perishest, perish there; if thou dost not, thou art sure to perish. If mercy be to be found anywhere, it is there. Herein appears Christ's· care to thee, that he hath given thee a heart in some degree sensible: he might have given thee up to hardness, security, and profaneness of heart, of all spiritual judgments the greatest. He that died for his enemies, will he refuse those, the desire of whose soul is towards him? He that by his messengers desires us to be reconciled, will he put us off when we earnestly seek it at his hand? No, doubtless, when he prevents us by kindling holy desires in us, he is ready to meet us in his own ways. When the prodigal set himself to return to his father, his father stays not for him, but meets him in the way. "When he prepares the heart to seek, he will cause his ear to hear," Ps. x. 17. He cannot find in his heart to hide himself long from us. If God should bring us into such a dark condition, as that we should see no light from himself, or the creature, then let us remember what he saith by the prophet Isaiah, "He that is in darkness, and seeth no light," Isa. l. 10, no light of comfort, no light of

God's countenance, "yet let him trust in the name of the Lord." We can never be in such a condition, wherein there will be just cause of utter despair; therefore let us do as mariners do, cast anchor in the dark. Christ knows how to pity us in this case; look what comfort he felt from his Father in his breakings, Isa. liii. 5, the like we shall feel from himself in our bruising.

The sighs of a bruised heart carry in them some report, as of our affection to Christ, so of his care to us. The eyes of our souls cannot be towards him, but that he hath cast a gracious look upon us first. The least love we have to him is but a reflection of his love first shining upon us. As Christ did in his example whatsoever he gives us in charge to do, so he suffered in his own person whatsoever he calleth us to suffer, that he might the better learn to relieve and pity us in our sufferings. In his desertion in the garden, and upon the cross, he was content to want that unspeakable solace in the presence of his Father, both to bear the wrath of the Lord for a time for us, and likewise to know the better how to comfort us in our greatest extremities. God seeth it fit we should taste of that cup of which his Son drank so deep, that we might feel a little what sin is, and what his Son's love was; but our comfort is, that Christ drank the dregs of the cup for us, and will succour us, that our spirits utterly fail not under that little taste of his displeasure which we may feel. He became not only a man, but a curse, a man of sorrows for us. He was broken, that we should not be broken; he was troubled, that we should not be desperately troubled; he became a curse, that we should not be accursed. Whatsoever may be wished for in an all-sufficient Comforter is all to be found in Christ, 1. Authority from the Father, all power was given him, Matt. xxviii. 18. 2. Strength in himself, as having his name the mighty God, Isa. ix. 6. 3. Wisdom, and that from his own experience, how and when to help. 4. Willingness, as being flesh of our flesh, and bone of our bone, Isa. ix. 6.

CHAP. XVII.—*Reproof of such as sin against this merciful disposition in Christ. Of quenching the Spirit.*

We are now to take notice of divers sorts of men that offend deeply against this merciful disposition of Christ: as, 1. Such as go on in all ill

courses of life upon this conceit, as if it were in
vain to go to Christ, their lives have been so ill;
whenas, so soon as we look to heaven, all encouragements are ready to meet us and draw us
forward.   Amongst others this is one allurement,
that Christ is ready to welcome us, and lead us
further.   None are damned in the church but
those that will.   Such as either enforce upon
themselves hard conceits of Christ, that they
may have some show of reason to fetch contentment from other things: as that unprofitable
servant, Matt. xxv. 30, that would needs take up
a conceit that his master was a hard man; here-
by to flatter himself in his unfruitful courses, in
not improving that talent which he had.

2. Such as take up a hope of their own, that
Christ will suffer them to walk in the ways to
hell, and yet bring them to heaven: whereas all
comfort should draw us nearer to Christ, else it
is a lying comfort, either in itself or in our
application of it.

And 3. Those that will cast water themselves
upon those sparks which Christ labours to kindle
in them, because they will not be troubled with
the light of them.

Such must know that the Lamb can be angry,
and they that will not come under his sceptre of

mercy, shall be crushed in pieces by his sceptre of power, Ps. ii. 9. Though he will graciously tender and maintain the least spark of true grace, yet where he findeth not the spark of grace, but opposition to his Spirit striving with them, his wrath once kindled shall burn to hell. There is no juster provocation than when kindness is churlishly refused.

When God would have cured Babylon, and she would not be cured, then she was given up to destruction, Jer. li. 9.

When Jerusalem would not be gathered under the wing of Christ, then their habitation is left desolate, Matt. xxiii, 37, 38.

When Wisdom stretcheth out her hand and men refuse, then Wisdom will laugh at men's destruction, Prov. i. 26.

Salvation itself will not save those that spill the potion, and cast away the plaster. A pitiful case, when this merciful Saviour shall delight in destruction: when he that made men shall have no mercy on them, Isa. xxvii. 11.

Oh, say the rebels of the time, God hath not made us to damn us. Yes, if you will not meet Christ in the ways of his mercy, it is fit you should "eat the fruit of your own ways, and be filled with your own devices," Prov. i. 31.

This will be the hell of hell, when men shall think, that they have loved their sins more than their souls ; when they shall think, what love and mercy hath been almost enforced upon them, and yet they would perish.   The more accessory we are in pulling a judgment upon ourselves, the more the conscience will be confounded in itself, when they shall acknowledge Christ to be without all blame, themselves without excuse.

If men appeal to their own consciences, they will tell them, the Holy Spirit hath often knocked at their hearts, as willing to have kindled some holy desires in them.   How else can they be said to resist the Holy Ghost, but that the Spirit was readier to draw them to a further degree of goodness than stood with their own wills ? whereupon those in the church that are damned are self-condemned before.   So that here we need not rise to higher causes, when men carry sufficient cause in their own bosoms.

4. And the best of us all may offend against this merciful disposition, if we be not watchful against that liberty our carnal disposition will be ready to take from it. Thus we reason, if Christ will not quench the smoking flax, what need we fear, that any neglect on our part can

bring us under a comfortless condition? If Christ will not do it, what can?

Ans. You know the apostle's prohibition notwithstanding, 1 Thess. v. 19, "Quench not the Spirit." These cautions of not quenching are sanctified by the Spirit as means of not quenching. Christ performeth his office in not quenching, by stirring up suitable endeavours in us; and none more solicitous in the use of the means than those that are most certain of the good success. The ground is this: the means that God hath set apart for the effecting of anything, fall under the same purpose that he hath to bring that thing to pass; and this is a principle taken for granted, even in civil matters; as who, if he knew before it would be a fruitful year, would therefore hang up his plough and neglect tillage?

Hence the apostle stirs up from the certain expectation of a blessing, 1 Cor. xv. 57, 58, and this encouragement here from the good issue of final victory is intended to stir us up, and not to take us off. If we be negligent in the exercise of grace received, and use of means prescribed, suffering our spirits to be oppressed with multitudes and variety of cares of this life, and take not heed of the damps of the times, for such miscarriage God in his wise care suffereth us oft to fall into a worse condition for feeling, than those that were never so much enlightened. Yet in mercy he will not suffer us to be so far enemies to ourselves, as wholly to neglect these sparks once kindled. Were it possible that we should be given up to give over all endeavour wholly, then we could look for no other issue but quenching; but Christ will tend this spark, and cherish this small seed, so as he will preserve in the soul always some degree of care. If we would make a comfortable use of this, we must consider all those means whereby Christ doth preserve grace begun; as *first*, holy communion, whereby one Christian heateth another; "two are better than one," etc., Eccles. iv. 9. "Did not our hearts burn?" Luke xxiv. 32, said the disciples. *Secondly*, much more communion with God in holy duties, as meditation and prayer, which doth not only kindle, but addeth a lustre to the soul. *Thirdly*, We feel by experience the breath of the Spirit to go along with the ministerial breath, whereupon the apostle knits these two together: "Quench not the Spirit;" "Despise not prophecies," 1 Thess. v. 19, 20. Nathan by a few words blew up the decaying sparks in David. Rather than God will suffer his fire in us to die he will send some Nathan or other, and something always is left in us to join with the word as connatural to it; as a coal that hath fire in it will quickly catch more to it: smoking flax will easily take fire. *Fourthly*, grace is strengthened by the exercise of it; "Up and be doing, and the Lord be with thee," 1 Chron. xxii. 16, said David to his son Solomon: stir up the grace that is in thee, for so holy motions turn to resolutions, resolutions to practice, and practice to a prepared readiness to every good work.

Caution. Yet let us know that grace is increased in the exercise of it, not by virtue of the exercise itself, but as Christ by his Spirit floweth into the soul, and bringeth us nearer unto himself the fountain, and instilleth such comfort in the act, whereby the heart is further enlarged. The heart of a Christian is Christ's garden, and his graces are as so many sweet spices and flowers, which his Spirit blowing upon makes them to send forth a sweet savour: therefore keep the soul open for entertainment of the Holy Ghost, for he will bring in continually fresh forces to subdue corruption, and this most of all on the Lord's day. John was in the Spirit on the Lord's day, even in Patmos, the place of his banishment, Rev. i. 10; then the gales of the

Spirit blow more strongly and sweetly. As we look, therefore, for the comfort of this doctrine, let us not favour our natural sloth, " but exercise ourselves to godliness," 1 Tim. iv. 7, and labour to keep this fire always burning upon the altar of our hearts, and dress our lamps daily, and put in fresh oil, and wind up our souls higher and higher still: resting in a good condition is contrary to grace, which cannot but promote itself to a further measure; let none turn this " grace into wantonness," Jude 4. Infirmities are a ground of humility, not a plea for negligence, not an encouragement to presumption. We should be so far from being ill, because Christ is good, as that those coals of love should melt us; therefore those may well suspect themselves in whom the consideration of this mildness of Christ doth not work that way: surely where grace is, corruption is as " smoke to their eyes, and vinegar to their teeth," Prov. x. 29. And therefore they will labour in regard of their own comfort, as likewise for the credit of religion, and the glory of God, that their light may break forth. If a spark of faith and love be so precious, what an honour will it be to be rich in faith! Who would not rather walk in the light, and in the comforts of the Holy Ghost, than to live in a dark perplexed estate? and not rather to be carried with full sail to heaven, than to be tossed always with fears and doubts? The present trouble in conflict against a sin is not so much as that disquiet which any corruption favoured will bring upon us afterward; true peace is in conquering, not in yielding. The comfort in this text intended is for those that would fain do better, but find their corruptions clog them; that are in such a mist, that ofttimes they cannot tell what to think of themselves; that fain would believe, and yet oft fear they do not believe, and think that it cannot be that God should be so good to such sinful wretches as they are; and yet they allow not themselves in these fears and doubts.

5. And among others, how do they wrong themselves and him, that will have other mediators to God for them than he? Are any more pitiful than he, who became man to that end, that he might be pitiful to his own flesh? Let all at all times repair to this meek Saviour, and put up all our suits in his prevailing name. What need we knock at any other door? can any be more tender over us than Christ? What encouragement have we to commend the state of the church in general, or of any broken-hearted Christian, unto him by our prayers? Of whom

we may speak unto Christ, as they of Lazarus, Lord, the church which thou lovest, and gavest thyself for, is in distress : Lord, this poor Christian, for whom thou wert bruised, Isa. liii. 5, is bruised and brought very low. It cannot but touch his bowels when the misery of his own dear bowels is spread before him.

6. Again, considering this gracious nature in Christ, let us think with ourselves thus: when he is so kind unto us, shall we be cruel against him in his name, in his truth, in his children ? how shall those that delight to be so terrible " to the meek of the earth," Zech. ii. 3, hope to look so gracious a Saviour in the face ? they that are so boisterous towards his spouse, shall know one day they had to deal with himself in his church. So it cannot but cut the heart of those that have felt this love of Christ, to hear him wounded who is the life of their lives, and the soul of their souls : this maketh those that have felt mercy weep over Christ, whom they have pierced with their sins. There cannot but be a mutual and quick sympathy between the head and the members. When we are tempted to any sin, if we will not pity ourselves, yet we should spare Christ, in not putting him to new torments. The apostle could not find out a more heart-breaking

argument to enforce a sacrificing ourselves to God, than to conjure us by the mercies of God in Christ, Rom. xii. 1.

7. This mercy of Christ likewise should move us to commiserate the state of the poor church, torn by enemies without, and rending itself by divisions at home. It cannot but work upon any soul that ever felt comfort from Christ, to consider what an affectionate entreaty the apostle useth to mutual agreement in judgment and affection. " If any consolation in Christ, if any comfort of love, if any fellowship of the Spirit, if any bowels and mercies, fulfil my joy, be like-minded," Phil. ii. 1 ; as if he should say, Unless you will disclaim all consolation in Christ, etc., labour to maintain the unity of the Spirit in the bond of peace. What a joyful spectacle is this to Satan and his faction, to see those that are separated from the world fall in pieces among themselves! Our discord is our enemy's melody.

The more to blame those that for private aims affect differences from others, and will not suffer the wounds of the church to close and meet together. Which must not be understood, as if men should dissemble their judgment in any truth where there is just cause of expressing themselves ; for the least truth is Christ's and not ours, and therefore we are not to take liberty to affirm or deny at our pleasures. There is a due in a penny as well as in a pound, therefore we must be faithful in the least truth, when season calleth for it. Then our "words are like apples of gold with pictures of silver," Prov. xxv. 11. One word spoken in season will do more good than a thousand out of season. But in some cases peace, by "keeping our faith to ourselves," Rom. xiv. 22, is of more consequence than the open discovery of some things we take to be true; considering the weakness of man's nature is such, that there can hardly be a discovery of any difference in opinion, without some estrangement of affection. So far as men are not of one mind, they will hardly be of one heart, except where grace and the peace of God, Col. iii. 15, bear great rule in the heart: therefore open show of difference is never good but when it is necessary; howsoever some, from a desire to be somebody, turn into by-ways, and yield to a spirit of contradiction in themselves; yet, if St. Paul may be judge, "are they not carnal?" 1 Cor. iii. 3; if it be wisdom, it is wisdom from beneath: for the wisdom from above, as it is pure, so it is peaceable, James iii. 17. Our blessed Saviour, when he was to leave the world, what doth he press upon his disciples more than peace and love? And in his last prayer, with what earnestness did he beg of his Father that "they might be one, as he and the Father were one!" John xvii. 21. But what he prayed for on earth, we shall only enjoy perfectly in heaven. Let this make the meditation of that time the more sweet unto us.

8. And further to lay open offenders in this kind, what spirit shall we think them to be of, that take advantages of the bruisedness and infirmities of men's spirits to relieve them with false peace for their own worldly ends? A wounded spirit will part with anything. Most of the gainful points of popery, as confession, satisfaction, merit, purgatory, etc., spring from hence, but they are physicians of no value, or rather tormentors than physicians at all. It is a greater blessing to be delivered from the "sting of these scorpions," Rev. ix. 5, than we are thankful for. Spiritual tyranny is the greatest tyranny, and then especially when it is where most mercy should be shewed ; yet even there some, like cruel surgeons, delight in making long cures, to serve themselves upon the misery of others. It bringeth men under a terrible curse, "when they will not remember

to shew mercy, but persecute the poor and needy man, that they might even slay the broken in heart," Ps. cix. 16.

Likewise, to such as raise temporal advantage to themselves out of the spiritual misery of others, join such as raise estates by betraying the church, and are unfaithful in the trust committed unto them: when the children shall cry for the bread of life, and there is none to give them, bringing thus upon the people of God that heavy judgment of a spiritual famine, starving Christ in his members; shall we so requite so good a Saviour, who counteth the love and mercy shewed " in feeding his lambs," John xxi. 15, as shewed to himself?

Last of all, they carry themselves very unkindly towards Christ, who stumble at this his low stooping unto us in his government and ordinances, that are ashamed of the simplicity of the gospel, that count preaching foolishness.

They, out of the pride of their heart, think they may do well enough without the help of the Word and Sacraments, and think Christ took not state enough upon him; and therefore they will mend the matter with their own devices, whereby they may give the better content to flesh and blood, as in popery. What greater unthankfulness can there be than to despise any help that Christ in mercy hath provided for us? In the days of his flesh, the proud Pharisees took offence at his familiar conversing with sinful men, who only did so as a physician to heal their souls. What defences was St. Paul driven to make for himself, for his plainness in unfolding the gospel? The more Christ, in himself and in his servants, shall descend to exalt us, the more we should, with all humility and readiness, entertain that love, and magnify the goodness of God, that hath put the great work of our salvation, and laid the government upon so gentle a Saviour, that will carry himself so mildly in all things wherein he is to deal betwixt God and us, and us and God. The lower Christ comes down to us, the higher let us lift him up in our hearts: so will all those do that have ever found the experience of Christ's work in their heart.

CHAP. XVIII.—*Of Christ's judgment in us, and his victory: what it is.*

We come to the third part, the constant progress of Christ's gracious power, until he hath set up such an absolute government in us, which shall prevail over all corruptions. It is said here, he will cherish his beginnings of grace in us, until he bring forth judgment unto victory. By judgment here, is meant the kingdom of grace in us, that government whereby Christ sets up a throne in our hearts. Governors among the Jews were first called judges, then kings : whence this inward rule is called judgment ; as likewise, because it agrees unto the judgment of the Word, which the psalmist oft calleth judgment, Ps. lxxii. 1, 2, because it agreeth to God's judgment. Men may read their doom in God's Word, what it judgeth of them God judgeth of them. By this judgment set up in us, good is discerned, allowed, and performed ; sin is judged, condemned, and executed. Our spirit being under the Spirit of Christ, is governed by him, and so far as it is governed by Christ, it governs us graciously.

Christ and we are of one judgment and of one will. He hath his will in us ; and his judgments are so invested into us, as that they are turned into our judgment, we carrying "his law in our hearts, written by his Spirit," Jer. xxxi. 33. The law in the inner man and the law written, answer as counterpanes each other.

The meaning then is, that the gracious frame of holiness set up in our hearts by the Spirit of Christ, shall go forward until all contrary power be brought under. The spirit of judgment will be a spirit of burning, Isa. iv. 4, to consume whatsoever opposed corruption like rust eats into the soul. If God's builders fall into errors, and build stubble upon a good foundation, God's Spirit as a spiritual "fire will reveal this in time," 1 Cor. iii. 13, and waste it. They shall, by a spirit of judgment, condemn their own errors and courses. The whole work of grace in us is set out under the name of judgment, and sometimes wisdom, because judgment is the chief and leading part in grace; whereupon that gracious work of repentance is called a change of the mind, and an after-wisdom. As on the other side, in the learned languages, the words that do express wisdom imply likewise the general relish and savour of the whole soul, and rather more the judgment of taste than of sight, or any other sense, because taste is the most necessary sense, and requireth the nearest application of the object of all other senses. So in spiritual life, it is most necessary that the Spirit should alter the taste of the soul, so as that it might savour the things of the Spirit so deeply, that all other things should be out of relish.

And as it is true of every particular Christian, that Christ's judgment in him shall be victorious, so likewise of the whole body of Christians—the Church. The government of Christ, and his truth, whereby he ruleth as by a sceptre, shall at length be victorious in spite of Satan, antichrist, and all enemies. Christ "riding on his white horse," Rev. vi. 2, hath a bow, and goeth forth conquering, Rev. xix. 11, in the ministry, that he may overcome either to conversion or to confusion. But yet I take judgment for Christ's kingdom and government within us principally. 1. Because God especially requireth the subjection of the soul and conscience as his proper throne. 2. Because if judgment should prevail in all other about us and not in our own hearts, it would not yield comfort to us; hereupon it is the first thing that we desire when we pray, " Thy kingdom come," that Christ would come and rule in our hearts. The kingdom of Christ in his ordinances serves but to bring Christ home into his own place, our hearts.

The words being thus explained, that judgment here includeth the government of both mind, will, and affections, there are divers conclusions that naturally do spring from them.

CHAP. XIX.—*Christ is so mild that yet he will govern those that enjoy the comfort of his mildness.*

The first conclusion from the connection of this part of the verse with the former is, that Christ is upon those terms mild, so that he will set up his government in those whom he is so gentle and tender over. He so pardons as he will be obeyed as a king; he so taketh us to be his spouse, as he will be obeyed as a husband. The same Spirit that convinceth us of the necessity of his righteousness to cover us, convinceth us also of the necessity of his government to rule us. His love to us moveth him to frame us to be like himself, and our love to him stirreth us up to be such as he may take delight in, neither have we any more faith or hope than care to be purged as he is pure; he maketh us subordinate governors, yea, kings under himself, giving us grace not only to set against, but to subdue in some measure our base affections. It is one main fruit of Christ's exaltation that he may turn every one of us from our wickedness, Acts iii. 26. " For this end Christ died and rose again and liveth, that he should be Lord of the dead and living," Rom. xiv. 9. God hath bound himself by an oath that he would grant us, that "without fear we might serve him in holiness and righteousness in his sight," Luke i. 75, not only in the sight of the world.

1. This may serve for a trial to discern who may lay just claim to Christ's mercy; only those that will take his yoke, and count it a greater happiness to be under his government, than to enjoy any liberty of the flesh; that will take whole Christ, and not single out of him what may stand with their present contentment; that will not divide Lord from Jesus, and so make a Christ of their own: none ever did truly desire mercy pardoning, but desired mercy healing. David prayeth for a new spirit, as well as for sense of pardoning mercy, Ps. li. 10.

2. This sheweth that those are misled, that make Christ to be only righteousness to us, and not sanctification, except by imputation: whereas it is a great part of our happiness to be under such a Lord, who was not only born for us, and given unto us, but "hath the government likewise upon his shoulders," Isa. ix. 6, 7, that is, our Sanctifier as well as our Saviour, our Saviour as well by the effectual power of his Spirit from the power of sin, as by the merit of his death from the guilt thereof; so that this (1.) Be re-

membered, that the first and chief ground of our comfort is, that Christ as a priest offered himself as a sacrifice to his Father for us. The guilty soul flieth first to Christ crucified, made a curse for us. Thence it is that Christ hath right to govern us, thence it is that he giveth us his Spirit as our guide to lead us home.

(2.) In the course of our life, after that we are in state of grace, and be overtaken with any sin, we must remember to have recourse first unto Christ's mercy to pardon us, and then to the promise of his Spirit to govern us.

(3.) And when we feel ourselves cold in affection and duty, it is the best way to warm ourselves at this fire of his love and mercy in giving himself for us.

(4.) Again, remember this, that Christ, as he ruleth us, so it is by a spirit of love from a sense of his love, whereby his commandments are easy to us. He leadeth us by his free Spirit, a Spirit of liberty: his subjects are voluntaries. The constraint that he layeth upon his subjects is that of love: he draweth us with the cords of love sweetly. Yet remember withal, that he draweth us strongly by a Spirit of power, for it is not sufficient that we have motives and encouragements to love and obey Christ from that love of his, whereby he gave himself for us to justify us*; but Christ's Spirit must likewise subdue our hearts, and sanctify them to love him, without which all motives would be ineffectual. Our disposition must be changed, we must be new creatures ; they seek for heaven in hell that seek for spiritual love in an unchanged heart, When a child obeys his father, it is so from reasons persuading him, as likewise from a childlike nature which giveth strength to these reasons : it is natural for a child of God to love Christ so far as he is renewed, not only from inducement of reason so to do, but likewise from an inward principle and work of grace, whence those reasons have their chief forces ; first, we are made partakers of the divine nature, and then we are easily induced and led by Christ's Spirit to spiritual duties.

CHAP. XX.—*The spiritual government of Christ is joined with judgment and wisdom.*

The second conclusion is, that Christ's government in his church and in his children is a wise and well-ordered government, because it is called judgment, and judgment is the life and soul of wisdom.   Of this conclusion there are two branches: 1. That the spiritual government of Christ in us is joined with judgment and wisdom. 2. Wheresoever true spiritual wisdom and judgment is, there likewise the Spirit of Christ bringeth in his gracious government. For the first, a well-guided life by the rules of Christ standeth with the strongest and highest reason of all; and therefore holy men are called the "children of wisdom," Luke vii. 31, and are able to justify, both by reason and experience, all the ways of wisdom. Opposite courses are folly and madness. Hereupon St. Paul saith, that a "spiritual man judgeth all things," 1 Cor. ii. 15, that appertain to him, and is judged of none that are of an inferior rank, because they want spiritual light and sight to judge; yet this sort of men will be judging, "and speaking ill of what they know not," 2 Pet. ii. 12; they step from ignorance to prejudice and rash censure, without taking right judgment in their way, and therefore their judgment comes to nothing. But the judgment of a spiritual man, so far forth as he is spiritual, shall stand, because it is agreeable to the nature of things: as things are in themselves, so they are in his judgment. As God is in himself infinite in goodness and majesty, etc., so he is to him; he ascribes to God in his heart his divinity and all his excellencies. As Christ is in himself the only Mediator, and all in all in the church, Col. iii. 11, so he is to him, by making Christ so in his heart. "As all things are dung in comparison of Christ," Phil. iii. 8, so they are to Paul, a sanctified man. As the very worst thing in religion, "the reproach of Christ is better than the pleasure of sin for a season," Heb. xi. 26; so it is to Moses, a man of a right esteem. "As one day in the courts of God is better than a thousand elsewhere," Ps. lxxxiv. 10, so it is to David, a man of a reformed judgment. There is a conformity of a good man's judgment to things as they are in themselves, and according to the difference or agreement put by God in things, so doth his judgment differ or agree.

Truth is truth, and error, error, and that which is unlawful is unlawful, whether men think so or no. God hath put an eternal difference betwixt light and darkness, good and ill, which no creature's conceit can alter; and therefore no man's judgment is the measure of things further than it agrees to truth stamped upon things themselves by God. Hereupon, because a wise man's judgment agrees to the truth of things, a wise man may in some sense be said to be the measure of things; and the judgment of one holy wise man to be preferred before a thousand others. Such men usually are immoveable as the sun in its course, because they think, and speak, and live by rule. "A Joshua and his house will serve God," Josh. xxiv. 15, whatsoever others do, and will run a course contrary to the world, because their judgments lead them a contrary way. Hence it is that Satan hath a spite at the eye of the soul, the judgment, to put out that by ignorance and false reason, for he cannot rule in any until either he hath taken away or perverted judgment: he is a prince of darkness, and ruleth in darkness of the understanding. Therefore he must first be cast out of the understanding by the prevailing of truth, and planting it in the soul. Those therefore that are enemies of knowledge help Satan and antichrist, whose kingdom, like Satan's, is a kingdom of darkness, to erect their throne. Hence it is promised by Christ, that "the Holy Ghost shall convince the world of judgment," John xvi. 8; that is, that he is resolved to set up a throne of government, because the great lord of misrule, "Satan, the prince of the world," is judged by the gospel, and the Spirit accompanying it, his impostures are discovered, his enterprises laid open; therefore when the gospel was spread, the oracles ceased, "Satan fell from heaven like lightning," Luke x. 18; men were "translated out of his kingdom into Christ's," Col. i. 13. Where prevailing is by lies, there discovery is victory; "they shall proceed no further, for their folly shall be manifest to all," 2 Tim. iii. 9. So that manifestation of error giveth a stop to it, for none will willingly be deceived. Let truth have full scope without check or restraint, and let Satan and his instruments do their worst, they shall not prevail; as Jerome saith of the Pelagians in his time. The discovery of your opinions is the vanquishing of them, your blasphemies appear at the first blush.

Use. Hence we learn the necessity, that the understanding be principled with supernatural knowledge, for the well managing of a Christian conversation.

There must be light to discover a further end than nature, for which we are Christians, and a rule suitable directing to that end, which is the will of God in Christ, discovering his good pleasure toward us, and our duty toward him; and in virtue of this discovery we do all that we do, that any way may further our reckoning: "The eye must first be single, and then the whole body and frame of our conversation will be light," Matt. vi. 22; otherwise both we and our course of life are nothing but darkness. The whole conversation of a Christian is nothing else but knowledge digested into will, affection, and practice. If the first concoction in the stomach be not good, that in the liver cannot be good ; so if there be error in the judgment, it mars the whole practice, as an error in the foundation doth the building : God will have " no blind sacrifices, no unreasonable services," Mal. i. 13, but will have us to " love him with all our mind," Rom. xii. 1, that is, with our understanding part as well as " with all our hearts," Luke x. 27, that is, the affecting part of the soul.

This order of Christ's government by judgment is agreeable unto the soul, and God delighteth to preserve the manner of working peculiar unto man, that is, to do what he doth out of judgment : as grace supposeth nature as founded upon it, so the frame of grace preserveth the frame of nature in man. And, therefore, Christ bringeth all that is good in the soul through judgment, and that so sweetly, that many out of a dangerous error think, that that good which is in them and issueth from them is from themselves, and not from the powerful work of grace. As in evil, the devil so subtilly leadeth us according to the stream of our own nature, that men think that

Satan had no hand in their sin ; but here a mistake
is with little peril, because we are ill of ourselves,
and the devil doth but promote what ill he findeth in us.   But there are no seeds of supernatural
goodness at all in us.   God findeth nothing in
us but enmity ; only he hath engraven this in
our nature to incline in general to that which we
judge to be good.'   Now when he shall clearly
discover what is good in particular, we are carried to it ; and when convincingly he shall discover that which is ill, we abhor it as freely as
we embraced it before.

From whence we may know, when we work as
we should do or no, that is, when we do what we
do out of inward principles, when we fall not
upon that which is good, only because we are so
bred, or because such or such whom we respect
do so, or because we will maintain a side, so
making religion a faction ; but out of judgment,
when what we do that is good, we first judge it
in ourselves so to be ; and what we abstain from
that is ill, we first judge it to be ill from an inward judgment.   A sound Christian, as he en-
joyeth the better part, so hath first made choice
of it with Mary, Luke x. 42 ; he established all
his thoughts by counsel, Prov. xx. 18.   God indeed useth carnal men to very good service, but

without a thorough altering and conviction of their judgment. He worketh by them, but not in them, therefore they do neither approve the good they do, nor hate the evil they abstain from.

CHAP. XXI.—*Where true wisdom and judgment is, there Christ sets up his government.*

The second branch is, that wheresoever true wisdom and judgment is, there Christ hath set up his government; because where wisdom is, it directs us not only to understand, but to order our ways aright. Where Christ by his Spirit as a prophet teaches, he likewise as a king by his Spirit subdueth the heart to obedience of what is taught. This is that teaching which is promised of God, when not only the brain, but the heart itself, is taught: when men do not only know what they should do, but are taught the very doing of it; they are not only taught that they should love, fear, and obey, but they are taught love itself, and fear and obedience itself. Christ sets up his chair in the very heart, and alters the frame of that, and makes his subjects good, together with teaching of them to be good. Other princes can make good laws, but they "cannot write them in their people's hearts," Jer. xxxii. 40. This is Christ's prerogative, he infuseth into his subjects his own Spirit, "Upon him there doth not only rest the spirit of wisdom and understanding, but likewise the Spirit of the fear of the Lord," Isa. xi. 2. The knowledge which we have of him from himself, is a transforming knowledge, 2 Cor. iii. 18. The same Spirit that enlighteneth the mind, inspireth gracious inclinations into the will and affections, and infuseth strength into the whole man. As a gracious man judgeth as he should, so he affecteth and doth as he judgeth, his life is a commentary of his inward man; there is a sweet harmony betwixt God's truth, his judgment, and his whole conversation. The heart of a Christian is like Jerusalem when it was at the best, a city compact within itself, Ps. cxii. 3; where are set up the thrones of judgment, Ps. cxxii. 5. Judgment should have a throne in the heart of every Christian. Not that judgment alone will work a change, there must be grace to alter the bent and sway of the will, before it will yield to be wrought upon by the understanding. But God hath so joined these together, as that whensoever he doth savingly shine upon the understanding, he giveth a soft and pliable heart; for without a work upon the heart by the Spirit of God, it will follow its own inclination to that which it affecteth, whatsoever the judgment shall say to the contrary : there is no connatural proportion betwixt an unsanctified heart and a sanctified judgment. For the heart unaltered will not give leave to the judgment coldly and soberly to conclude what is best : as the sick man whilst his aguish distemper corrupteth his taste, is rather desirous to please that, than to hearken what the physician shall speak. Judgment hath not power over itself where the will is unsubdued, for the will and affections bribe it to give sentence for them, when any profit or pleasure shall come in competition with that which the judgment in general only shall think to be good ; and, therefore, it is for the most part in the power of the heart, what the understanding shall judge and determine in particular things. Where grace hath brought the heart under, there unruly passions do not cast such a mist before the understanding, but that in particular it seeth that which is best; and base respects, springing from self-love, do not alter the case, and bias the judgment into a contrary way ; but that which is good in itself shall be good unto us, although it cross our particular worldly interests.

Use. The right conceiving of this hath an influence into practice, which hath drawn me to a more full explanation: this will teach us the right method of godliness, to begin with judgment, and then to beg of God, together with illumination, holy inclinations of our will and affections, that so a perfect government may be set up in our hearts, and that our "knowledge may be with all judgment," Phil. i. 9; that is, with experience and feeling. When the judgment of Christ is set up in our judgments, and thence, by the Spirit of Christ, brought into our hearts, then it is in its proper place and throne; and until then, truth doth us no good, but helpeth to condemn us. The life of a Christian is a regular life, and he that walketh by the rule, Gal. vi. 16, of the new creature, peace shall be upon him: "he that despiseth his way and loveth to live at large, seeking all liberty to the flesh, shall die," Prov. xix. 16. And it is made good by St. Paul, "If we live after the flesh, we shall die," Rom. viii. 13.

We learn likewise that men of an ill-governed life have no true judgment: no wicked man can be a wise man. And that without Christ's Spirit the soul is in confusion, without beauty and form, as all things were in the chaos before the creation. The whole soul is out of joint till it be set in again by him whose office is to "restore all things." The baser part of the soul which should be subject, ruleth all, and keepeth under that little truth that is in the understanding, holding it captive to base affections; and Satan by corruption getteth all the holds of the soul, till Christ, stronger than he, cometh, and driveth him out, and taketh possession of all the powers and parts of soul and body, to be weapons of righteousness, to serve him, and then new lords new laws. Christ as a new conqueror changeth the fundamental laws of old Adam, and establisheth a government of his own.

CHAP. XXII.—*Christ's government is victorious.*

The third conclusion is, that this government is victorious. The reasons are:—

1. Because Christ hath conquered all in his own person first, and he is God over all, blessed for evermore; and therefore over "sin, death, hell, Satan, the world," etc., Rom. ix. 5. And as he hath overcome them in himself, so he overcomes them in our hearts and consciences. We used to say, conscience maketh a man a king or a caitiff, because it is planted in us to judge for

God, either with us or against us. Now if natural conscience be so forcible, what will it be when besides its own light it hath the light of divine truth put into it? It will undoubtedly prevail, either to make us hold up our heads with boldness, or abase us beneath ourselves. If it subject itself by grace to Christ's truth, then it boldly overlooks death, hell, judgment, and all spiritual enemies, because then Christ sets up his kingdom in the conscience, and makes it a kind of paradise.

The sharpest conflict which the soul hath is between the conscience and God's justice: now if the conscience, sprinkled with the blood of Christ, hath prevailed over assaults fetched from the justice of God as now satisfied by Christ, it will prevail over all other opposition whatsoever.

2. We are to encounter with accursed and damned enemies; therefore if they begin to fall before the Spirit in us, they shall fall: if they rise up again, it is to have the greater fall.

3. The Spirit of truth, to whose tuition Christ hath committed his church, and the truth of the Spirit, which is the sceptre of Christ, abide for ever; therefore the soul begotten by the immortal seed of the Spirit, 1 Pet. i. 23, and this truth, must not only live for ever, but likewise

prevail over all that oppose it, for both the Word and Spirit are mighty in operation, Heb. iv. 12; and if the ill spirit be never idle in those whom God delivereth up to him, we cannot think that the Holy Spirit will be idle in those whose leading and government is committed to him. No; as he dwelleth in them, so he will drive out all that rise up against him, until he be all in all.

What is spiritual is eternal. Truth is a beam of Christ's Spirit, both in itself and as it is ingrafted into the soul, therefore it, and the grace, though little, wrought by it, will prevail. A little thing in the hand of a giant will do great matters. A little faith strengthened by Christ will work wonders.

4. "To him that hath shall be given," Matt. xxv. 29; the victory over any corruption or temptation is a pledge of final victory. As Joshua said when he set his foot upon the five kings which he conquered, "Thus God shall do with all our enemies," Josh. x. 25; heaven is ours already, only we strive till we have full possession.

5. Christ as king brings in a commanding light into the soul, and bows the neck, and softens the iron sinew of the inner man; and

where he begins to rule, he rules for ever, "his kingdom hath no end," Luke i. 33.

6. The end of Christ's coming was to destroy the works of the devil, both for us and in us; and the end of the resurrection was, as to seal unto us the assurance of his victory; so, 1, To quicken our souls from death in sin; 2, To free our souls from such snares and sorrows of spiritual death as accompany the guilt of sin; 3, To raise them up more comfortable, as the sun breaks forth more gloriously out of a thick cloud; 4, To raise us out of particular slips and failings, stronger; 5, To raise us out of all troublesome and dark conditions of this life; and, 6, At length to raise our bodies out of the dust. For the same power that the Spirit showed in raising Christ, our head, from the sorrows of death, and the lowest degree of his abasement; the same power obtained by the death of Christ from God, now appeased by that sacrifice, will the Spirit show in the church, which is his body, and in every particular member thereof.

And this power is conveyed by faith, whereby, after union with Christ in both his estates of humiliation and exaltation, we see ourselves not only "dead with Christ, but risen and sitting together with him in heavenly places," Eph. ii.

6. Now we, apprehending ourselves to be dead and risen, and thereupon victorious over all our enemies in our head, and apprehending that his scope in all this is to conform us to himself, we are by this faith changed into his likeness, 2 Cor. iii. 18, and so become conquerors over all our spiritual enemies, as he is, by that power which we derive from him, who is the storehouse of all spiritual strength for all his. Christ at length will have his end in us, and faith resteth assured of it, and this assurance is very operative, stirring us up to join with Christ in his ends.

And so for the church in general, by Christ it will have its victory: Christ is "that little stone cut out of the mountain without hands, that breaketh in pieces that goodly image," Dan. ii. 35, that is, all opposite government, until it become "a great mountain, and filleth the whole earth." So that the stone that was cut out of the mountain, becomes a mountain itself at length. Who art thou, then, O mountain, that thinkest to stand up against this mountain? All shall lie flat and level before it: he will bring down all mountainous, high, exalted thoughts, and lay the pride of all flesh low. When chaff strives against the wind, stubble against the fire, when the heel kicks against the pricks, when the potsherd strives with the potter, when man strives against God, it is easy to know on which side the victory will go. The winds may toss the ship wherein Christ is, but not overturn it. The waves may dash against the rock, but they do but break themselves against it.

Object. If this be so, why is it thus with the church of God, and with many a gracious Christian? the victory seemeth to go with the enemy.

Ans. For answer, remember, 1, God's children usually in their troubles overcome by suffering; here lambs overcome lions, and doves eagles, by suffering, that herein they may be conformable to Christ, who conquered most when he suffered most; together with Christ's kingdom of patience there was a kingdom of power.

2. This victory is by degrees, and therefore they are too hasty spirited that would conquer so soon as they strike the first stroke, and be at the end of their race at the first setting forth; the Israelites were sure of their victory in their voyage to Canaan, yet they must fight it out. God would not have us presently forget what cruel enemies Christ hath overcome for us; "Destroy them not, lest the people forget it," saith the Psalmist, Ps. lix. 11. That so by the

experience of that annoyance we have by them, we might be kept in fear to come under the power of them.

3. That God often worketh by contraries: when he means to give victory, he will suffer us to be foiled at first; when he means to comfort, he will terrify first; when he means to justify, he will condemn us first; whom he means to make glorious, he will abase first. A Christian conquers, even when he is conquered; when he is conquered by some sins, he gets victory over others more dangerous, as spiritual pride, security, etc.

4. That Christ's work, both in the church and in the hearts of Christians, often goeth backward, that it may go the better forward. As seed rots in the ground in the winter time, but after comes better up, and the harder the winter, the more flourishing the spring, so we learn to stand by falls, and get strength by weakness discovered— *virtutis custos infirmitas*—we take deeper root by shaking; and, as torches flame brighter by moving, thus it pleaseth Christ, out of his freedom, in this manner to maintain his government in us. Let us herein labour to exercise our faith, that it may answer Christ's manner of carriage towards us; when we are foiled, let us

believe we shall overcome; when we are fallen,
let us believe we shall rise again. Jacob, after
he had a " blow upon which he halted, yet would
not give over wrestling," Gen. xxxii. 24, till he
had gotten the blessing; so let us never give
over, but in our thoughts knit the beginning,
progress, and end together, and then we shall
see ourselves in heaven out of the reach of all
enemies. Let us assure ourselves that God's
grace, even in this imperfect state, is stronger
than man's free will in the state of first perfection, being founded now in Christ, who, as he is
the author, so will be " the finisher of our faith,"
Heb. xii. 2 ; we are under a more gracious covenant.

That which some say of faith rooted, *fides
radicata*, that it continueth, but weak faith may
come to nothing, seemeth to be crossed by this
Scripture; for, as the strongest faith may be
shaken, so the weakest where truth is, is so far
rooted, that it will prevail. Weakness with
watchfulness will stand out, when strength with
too much confidence faileth. Weakness, with
acknowledging of it, is the fittest seat and subject for God to perfect his strength in ; for consciousness of our infirmities driveth us out of
ourselves to him in whom our strength lieth.

Hereupon it followeth that weakness may stand with the assurance of salvation; the disciples, notwithstanding all their weaknesses, are bidden to rejoice, Luke x. 20, that their names are written in heaven. Failings, with conflict, in sanctification should not weaken the peace of our justification, and assurance of salvation. It mattereth not so much what ill is in us, as what good; not what corruptions, but how we stand affected to them; not what our particular failings be, so much as what is the thread and tenor of our lives; for Christ's mislike of that which is amiss in us, redounds not to the hatred of our persons, but to the victorious subduing of all our infirmities.

Some have, after conflict, wondered at the goodness of God, that so little and shaking faith should have upheld them in so great combats, when Satan had almost catched them. And, indeed, it is to be wondered how much a little grace will prevail with God for acceptance, and over our enemies for victory, if the heart be upright. Such is the goodness of our sweet Saviour, that he delighteth still to shew his strength in our weakness.

Use 1. First, therefore, for the great consolation of poor and weak Christians, let them know, that a spark from heaven, though kindled under greenwood that sobs and smokes, yet it will consume all at last. Love once kindled is strong as death, much water cannot quench it, and therefore it is called a vehement flame, or flame of God, Cant. viii. 6, kindled in the heart by the Holy Ghost; that little that is in us is fed with an everlasting spring. As the fire that came down from heaven in Elias' time, 1 Kings xviii. 38, licked up all the water, to shew that it came from God, so will this fire spend all our corruption; no affliction without, or corruption within, shall quench it. In the morning we see oft clouds gather about the sun, as if they would hide it, but the sun wasteth them by little and little, till it come to its full strength. At the first, fears and doubts hinder the breaking out of this fire, until at length it gets above them all, and Christ prevails; and then he backs his own graces in us. Grace conquers us first, and we by it conquer all things else; whether it be corruptions within us or temptations without us.

The church of Christ, begotten by the word of truth, hath the doctrine of the apostles for her crown, and tramples the moon, that is, the world, and all worldly things, "under her feet," Rev. xii. 1; "every one that is born of God overcometh the world," 1 John v. 4. Faith, whereby especially Christ rules, sets the soul so high, that it overlooks all other things as far below, as having represented to it, by the Spirit of Christ, riches, honour, beauty, pleasures of a higher nature.

Now that we may not come short of the comfort intended, there are two things especially to be taken notice of by us: 1. Whether there be such a judgment or government set up in us, to which this promise of victory is made. 2. Some rules or directions how we are to carry ourselves, that the judgment of Christ in us may indeed be victorious.

The evidences whereby we may come to know that Christ's judgment in us is such as will be victorious are, 1. If we be able from experience to justify all Christ's ways, let flesh and blood say what it can to the contrary, and can willingly subscribe to that course which God hath taken in Christ, to bring us to heaven, and still approve a further measure of grace than we have attained unto, and project and forecast for it. No other man can justify their courses, when their conscience is awaked. 2. When reasons of religion be the strongest reasons with us, and prevail more than reasons fetched from worldly policy.

3. When we are so true to our ends and fast to our rule, as no hopes or fears can sway us another way, but still we are looking what agrees or differs from our rule.   4. When we " can do nothing against the truth, but for the truth," 2 Cor. xiii. 8, as being dearer to us than our lives ; truth hath not this sovereignty in the heart of any carnal man.   5. When if we had liberty to choose under whose government we would live, yet out of a delight in the inner man to Christ's government we would make choice of him only to rule us before any other, for this argues, that we are like-minded to Christ, a free and a voluntary people, and not compelled unto Christ's service, otherwise than by the sweet constraint of love.   When we are so far in liking with the government of Christ's Spirit, that we are willing to resign up ourselves to him in all things, for then his kingdom is come unto us, when our wills are brought to his will.   It is the bent of our wills that maketh us good or ill.

6. A well-ordered uniform life, not by fits or starts, shews a well-ordered heart, as in a clock when the hammer strikes well, and the hand of the dial points well, it is a sign that the wheels are right set.   7. When Christ's will cometh in competition with any earthly loss or gain, yet if

then, in that particular case, the heart will stoop to Christ, it is a true sign ; for the truest trial of the power of grace is in such particular cases which touch us nearest, for there our corruption maketh the greatest head. When Christ came near home to the young man, Matt. x. 22, in the gospel, he lost a disciple of him. 8. When we can practise duties pleasing to Christ, though contrary to flesh, and the course of the world, and when we can overcome ourselves in that evil to which our nature is prone, and standeth so much inclined unto, and which agreeth to the sway of the times, and which others lie enthralled under, as desire of revenge, hatred of enemies, private ends, etc., then it appears that grace is in us above nature, heaven above earth, and will have the victory.

For the further clearing of this and helping of us in our trial, we must know there be three degrees of victory. 1. When we resist though we be foiled. 2. When grace gets the better though with conflict. 3. When all corruption is perfectly subdued. Now we have strength but only to resist, yet we may know Christ's government in us will be victorious, because what is said of the devil is said of all our spiritual enemies, " if we resist they shall in time fly from us," James iv. 7 ; because "stronger is he that is in us," that taketh part with his own grace, "than he that is in the world," 1 John iv. 4. And if we may hope for victory upon bare resistance, what may we not hope for when the Spirit hath gotten the upper hand ?

CHAP. XXIII.—*Means to make Grace victorious.*

For the second, that is, directions.

We must know, though Christ hath undertaken this victory, yet he accomplished it by training us up to fight his battles ; he overcometh in us, by making us "wise to salvation," 2 Tim. iii. 15 ; and in what degree we believe Christ will conquer, in that degree we will endeavour by his grace that we may conquer; for faith is an obedient and a wise grace. Christ maketh us wise to ponder and weigh things, and thereupon to rank and order them so as we may make the fitter choice of what is best. Some rules to help us in judging are these :

(1.) To judge of things as they help or hinder the main ; (2.) as they further or hinder our reckoning ; (3.) as they make us more or, less spiritual, and so bring us nearer to the fountain of goodness, God himself ; (4.) as they bring us peace or sorrow at the last; (5.) as they commend us more or less to God, and wherein we shall approve ourselves to him most; (6.) likewise to judge of things now, as we shall do hereafter when the soul shall be best able to judge, as when we are under any public calamity, or at the hour of death, when the soul gathereth itself from all other things to itself; (7.) look back to former experience, see what is most agreeable unto it, what was best in our worst times. If grace is or was best then, it is best now. And (8.) labour to judge of things as he doth who must judge us, and as holy men judge, who are led by the Spirit; more particularly, (9.) what those judge, that have no interest in any benefit that may come by the thing which is in question: for outward things blind the eyes even of the wise; we see papists are most corrupt in those things where their honour, ease, or profit is engaged; but in the doctrine of the Trinity, which doth not touch upon these things, they are sound. But it is not sufficient that judgment be right, but likewise ready and strong.

1. Where Christ establisheth his government, he inspireth care to keep the judgment clear and fresh, for whilst the judgment standeth straight and firm, the whole frame of the soul continueth

strong and impregnable. True judgment in us advanceth Christ, and Christ will advance it. All sin is either from false principles, or ignorance, or mindlessness, or unbelief of true. By inconsideration and weakness of assent, Eve lost her hold at first, Gen. iii. 6. It is good, therefore, to store up true principles in our hearts, and to refresh them often, that in virtue of them our affections and actions may be more vigorous. When judgment is fortified, evil finds no entrance, but good things have a side within us, to entertain them. Whilst true convincing light continueth, we will not do the least ill of sin for the greatest ill of punishment. "In vain is the net spread in the eyes of that which hath wings," Prov. i. 17. Whilst the soul is kept aloft, there is little danger of snares below; we lose our high estimation of things before we can be drawn to any sin.

2. And because knowledge and affection mutually help one another, it is good to keep up our affections of love and delight, by all sweet inducements and divine encouragements; for what the heart liketh best, the mind studieth most. Those that can bring their hearts to delight in Christ know most of his ways. Wisdom loveth him that loves her. Love is the best entertainer

of truth; and when it is not "entertained in the love of it," 2 Thess. ii. 10, being so lovely as it is, it leaveth the heart, and will stay no longer. It hath been a prevailing way to begin by withdrawing the love to corrupt the judgment; because as we love, so we use to judge; and therefore it is hard to be affectionate and wise in earthly things; but in heavenly things, where there hath been a right information of the judgment before, the more our affections grow, the better and clearer our judgments will be, because our affections, though strong, can never rise high enough to the excellency of the things. We see in the martyrs, when the sweet doctrine of Christ had once gotten their hearts, it could not be gotten out again by all the torments the wit of cruelty could devise. If Christ hath once possessed the affections, there is no dispossessing of him again. A fire in the heart overcometh all fires without.

3. Wisdom likewise teacheth us wherein our weakness lieth, and our enemy's strength, whereby a jealous fear is stirred up in us, whereby we are preserved; for out of this godly jealousy we keep those provocations which are active and working, from that which is passive and catching in us, as we keep fire from powder. They that will hinder

the generation of noisome creatures, will hinder
the conception first, by keeping male and female
asunder.   This jealousy will be much furthered
by observing strictly what hath helped or hindered a gracious temper in us ; and it will make
us take heed that we consult not with flesh and
blood in ourselves or others. How else can
we think that Christ will lead us out to
victory, when we take counsel of his and our
enemies ?

4. Christ maketh us likewise careful to attend
all means whereby fresh thoughts and affections
may be stirred up and preserved in us. Christ
so honoureth the use of means, and the care he
putteth into us, that he ascribeth both preserva-
tion and victory unto our care of keeping ourselves. "He that is begotten of God keepeth
himself," 1 John v. 18 ; but not by himself, but
by the Lord, in dependence on him on the use
of means. We are no longer safe than wise to
present ourselves to all good advantages of
acquaintance, etc. By going out of God's walks
we go out of his government, and so lose our
frame, and find ourselves overspread quickly with
a contrary disposition. When we draw near to
Christ, ·James iv. 8, in his ordinances he draws
near unto us.

5. Keep grace in exercise. It is not sleepy habits, but grace in exercise, that preserveth us. Whilst the soul is in some civil or sacred employment, corruptions within us are much suppressed, and Satan's passages stopped, and the Spirit hath a way open to enlarge itself in us, and likewise the guard of angels then most nearly attends us; which course often prevails more against our spiritual enemies than direct opposition. It stands upon Christ's honour to maintain those that are in his work.

6. Sixthly, in all directions we must look up to Christ the quickening Spirit, and resolve in his strength. Though we are exhorted "to cleave to the Lord with full purpose of heart," Acts xi. 23, yet we must pray with David, "Lord, for ever keep it in the thoughts of our hearts, and prepare our hearts unto thee," 1 Chron. xxix. 13. Our hearts are of themselves very loose and unsettled, "Lord, unite our hearts unto thee to fear thy name," Ps. lxxxvi. 11; or else, without him, our best purposes will fall to the ground. It is a pleasing request, out of love to God, to beg such a frame of soul from him, wherein he may take delight; and, therefore, in the use of all the means we must send up our desires and complaints to heaven to him for

strength and help, and then we may be sure that "he will bring forth judgment unto victory."

7. Lastly, it furthers the state of the soul, to know what frame it should be in, that'so we may order our souls accordingly. We should always be fit for communion with God, and be heavenly-minded in earthly business, and be willing to be taken off from them, to redeem time for better things. We should be ready at all times to depart hence, and to live in such a condition as we would be content to die in. We should have hearts prepared for every good duty, open to all good occasions, and shut to all temptations, keeping our watch, and being always ready armed. So far as we come short of these things, so far we have just cause to be humbled, and yet press forward, that we may gain more upon ourselves, and make these things more familiar and lovely unto us; and when we find our souls anyways falling downwards, it is best to raise them up presently by some waking meditations, as of the presence of God, of the strict reckoning we are to make, of the infinite love of God in Christ, and the fruits of it, of the excellency of a Christian's calling, of the short and uncertain time of this life; how little good all those things that steal away our hearts will

do us ere long, and how it shall be for ever with us thereafter, as we spend this little time well or ill, etc. The more we give way for such considerations to sink into our hearts, the more we shall rise nearer to that state of soul which we shall enjoy in heaven. When we grow regardless of keeping our souls, then God recovers our taste of good things again by sharp crosses. Thus David, Solomon, Samson, etc., were recovered. It is much easier kept than recovered.

Object. But, notwithstanding my striving, I seem to stand at a stay.

Ans. 1. Grace, as the seed in the parable, grows, we know not how, yet at length, when God seeth fittest, we shall see that all our endeavour hath not been in vain. The tree falleth upon the last stroke, yet all the former strokes help it forward.

Ans. 2. Sometimes victory is suspended because some Achan is not found out, Judges xx. 26 ; or because we are not humble enough, as Israel had the worst against the Benjamites till they fasted and prayed ; or because we betray our helps, and stand not upon our guard, and yield not presently to the motions of the Spirit, which mindeth us always of the best things, if we would regard it. Our own consciences will tell us, if we give them leave to speak, that some sinful favouring of ourselves is the cause. The way in this case to prevail is, 1, To get the victory over the pride of our own nature, by taking shame to ourselves, in humble confession to God; and then, 2, To overcome the unbelief of our hearts, by yielding to the promise of pardon; and then, 3, In confidence of Christ's assistance, to set ourselves against those sins which have prevailed over us; and then prevailing over ourselves, we shall easily prevail over all our enemies, and conquer all conditions we shall be brought into.

CHAP. XXIV.—*All should side with Christ.*

Use 2. If Christ will have the victory, then it is the best way for nations and states to "kiss the Son," Ps. ii. 12, and to embrace Christ and his religion, to side with Christ, and to own his cause in the world. His side will prove the stronger side at last. Happy are we if Christ honour us so much as to use our help "to fight his battle against the mighty," Judges v. 23. True religion in a state is as the main pillar of a house, and staff of a tent that upholds all. 2. So for families, let Christ be the chief governor of the family; and, 3. Let every one be as a house of Christ, to dwell familiarly in, and to rule. Where Christ is, all happiness must follow. If Christ goeth, all will go. Where Christ's government in his ordinances and his Spirit is, there all subordinate government will prosper. Religion inspireth life and grace into all other things; all other virtues, without it they are but as a fair picture without a head. Where Christ's laws are written in the heart, there all other good laws are best obeyed. None despise man's law but those that despise Christ's first. *Nemo humanam authoritatem contemnit, nisi qui divinam prius contempsit.* Of all persons, a man guided by Christ is the best; and of all creatures in the world, a man guided by will and affection, next the devil, is the worst. The happiness of weaker things stands in being ruled by stronger. It is best for a blind man to be guided by him that hath sight; it is best for sheep, and such like shiftless creatures, to be guided by man; and it is happiest for man to be guided by Christ, because his government is so victorious that it frees us from the fear and danger of our greatest enemies, and tends to bring us to the greatest happiness that our nature is capable of. This should make us to joy when Christ reigneth in us. When " Solomon was crowned the people shouted," so that the " earth rang," 1 Kings i. 39, 40. Much more should we rejoice in Christ our King.

And likewise for those whose souls are dear unto us, our endeavour should be that Christ may reign in them also, that they may be baptised by Christ with this fire, Matt. iii. 11, that these sparks may be kindled in them. Men labour to cherish the spirit and mettle, as they term it, of those they train up, because they think they will have use of it in the manifold affairs and troubles of this life. Oh, but let us cherish the sparks of grace in them ; for a natural spirit in great troubles will fail, but these sparks will make them conquerors over the greatest evils.

Use 3. If Christ's judgment shall be victorious, then popery, being an opposite frame, set up by the wit of man to maintain stately idleness, must fall. And it is fallen already in the hearts of those upon whom Christ hath shined. It is a lie, and founded upon a lie, upon the infallible judgment of a man subject to sin and error. When that which is taken for a principle of truth becomes a principle of error, the more relying upon it, the more danger.

CHAP. XXV.—*Christ's government shall be openly victorious.*

It is not only said, *judgment shall be victorious, but that Christ will bring it openly forth to victory.* Whence we observe, that grace shall be glory, and run into the eyes of all. Now Christ doth conquer, and hath his own ends, but it is in some sort invisibly. His enemies within and without us seem to have the better. But he will bring forth judgment unto victory, to the view of all. The wicked that now shut their eyes shall see it to their torment. It shall not be in the power of subtle men to see or not see what they would. Christ will have power over their hearts; and as his wrath shall immediately seize upon their souls against their wills, so will he have power over the eyes of their souls, to see and know what will increase their misery. Grief shall be fastened to all their senses, and their senses to grief.

Then all the false glosses which they put upon things shall be wiped off. Men are desirous to have the reputation of good, and yet the sweetness of ill; nothing so cordially opposed by them, as that truth which layeth them open to themselves, and to the eyes of others, their chief care

being how to daub with the world and their own
consciences. But the time will come when they
shall be driven out of this fools' paradise, and the
more subtle their conveyance of things hath been,
the more shall be their shame. Christ, whom
God hath chosen to set forth the chief glory of
his excellencies, is now veiled in regard of his
body the church, but will come ere long to be
glorious in his saints, 2 Thess. i. 10, and not lose
the clear manifestation of any of his attributes ;
and will declare to all the world what he is, when
there shall be no glory but that of Christ and his
spouse. Those that are as smoking flax now
shall then " shine as the sun in the firmament,"
Matt. xiii. 43, and their " righteousness break
forth as the noon-day," Ps. xxxvii. 6.

The image of God in Adam had a commanding majesty in it, so that all creatures reverenced
him ; much more shall the image of God in the
perfection of it command respect in all. Even
now there is a secret awe put into the hearts of
the greatest, towards those in whom they see any
grace to shine, from whence it was that Herod
feared John Baptist ; but what will this be in
their day of bringing forth, which is called " the
day of the revelation of the sons of God ?" Rom.
viii. 19.

There will be more glorious times when " the kingdoms of the earth shall be the Lord Jesus Christ's," Rev. xi. 10, and he shall reign for ever; then shall judgment and truth have its victory; then Christ will plead his own cause; truth shall no longer be called heresy and schism, nor heresy catholic doctrine; wickedness shall no longer go masked and disguised; goodness shall appear in its own lustre, and shine in its own beams; things shall be what they are, " nothing is hidden but shall be laid open," Matt. x. 26; iniquity shall not be carried in a mystery any longer; deep dissemblers, that think to hide their counsels from the Lord, shall walk no longer invisible as in the clouds. As Christ will not quench the least spark kindled by himself, so will he damp the fairest blaze of goodly appearances which are not from above.

Use. If this were believed, men would make more account of sincerity, which will only give us boldness, and not seek for covershames; the confidence whereof, as it maketh men now more presumptuous, so it will expose them hereafter to the greater shame.

If judgment shall be brought forth to victory, then those that have been ruled by their own deceitful hearts and a spirit of error, shall be brought forth to disgrace; that God that hath joined grace and truth with honour, hath joined sin and shame together at last; all the wit and power of man can never be able to sever what God hath coupled. Truth and piety may be trampled upon for a time, but as the two witnesses, Rev. xi. 11, after they were slain rose again, and stood upon their feet, so whatsoever is of God shall at length stand upon its own bottom. There shall be a resurrection not only of bodies but of credits. Can we think that he that threw the angels out of heaven will suffer dust and worm's meat to run a contrary course, and to carry it always so? No; as verily as Christ is " King of kings, and Lord of lords," Rev. xix. 16, so will he dash all those pieces of earth " which rise up against him as a potter's vessel," Ps. ii. 9. Was there ever any fierce against God and prospered? Job ix. 4. No; doubtless the rage of man shall turn to Christ's praise, Ps. lxxvi. 10. What was said of Pharaoh shall be said of all heady enemies, who had rather lose their souls than their wills, that they are but raised up for Christ to get himself glory in their confusion.

Let us, then, take heed that we follow not the ways of those men, whose ends we shall tremble at; there is not a more fearful judgment can befall the nature of man, than to be given up to a reprobate judgment of persons and things, because it cometh under a woe " to call ill good, and good ill," Isa. v. 20.

How will they be laden with curses another day that abuse the judgment of others by sophistry and flattery, deceivers, and being deceived? 2 Tim. iii. 13. Then the complaint of our first mother Eve will be taken up but fruitlessly, Gen. xiii. 3; the serpent hath deceived me; Satan in such and such hath deceived me; sin hath deceived me; a foolish heart hath deceived me. It is one of the highest points of wisdom to consider upon what grounds we venture our souls. Happy men will they be, who have by Christ's light a right judgment of things, and suffer that judgment to prevail over their hearts.

The soul of most men is drowned in their senses, and carried away with weak opinions, raised from vulgar mistakes and shadows of things. And Satan is ready to enlarge the imagination of outward good and outward ill, and make it greater than it is, and spiritual things less, presenting them through false glasses. And so men, trusting in vanity, vanquish themselves in their own apprehensions. A woful condition, when both we and that which we highly esteem shall vanish together, which will be as truly as Christ's judgment shall come to victory; and in what measure the vain heart of man hath been enlarged, to conceive a greater good in things of this world than there is, by so much the soul shall be enlarged to be more sensible of misery when it sees its error. This is the difference betwixt a godly wise man and a deluded worldling; that which the one doth now judge to be vain, the other shall hereafter feel to be so when it is too late. But this is the vanity of our natures, that though we shun above all things to be deceived and mistaken in present things, yet in the greatest matters of all we are willingly ignorant and misled.

CHAP. XXVI.—*Christ alone advanceth this government.*

The fifth conclusion is, that this government is set up and advanced by Christ alone; he bringeth judgment to victory. We both fight and prevail "in the power of his might," Eph. vi. 10; we overcome by the spirit obtained by "the blood of the Lamb," Rev. xii. 11.

It is *he* alone that "teacheth our hands to war,

and fingers to fight," Ps. cxliv. 1. Nature, as corrupted, favours its own being, and will maintain itself against Christ's government. Nature, simply considered, cannot raise itself above itself to actions spiritual of a higher order and nature; therefore the divine power of Christ is necessary to carry us above all our own strength, especially in duties wherein we meet with greater opposition; for there not only nature will fail us, but ordinary grace, unless there be a stronger and a new supply. In taking up a burden that is weightier than ordinary, if there be not a greater proportion of strength than weight, the undertaker will lie under it; so to every strong encounter there must be a new supply of strength, as in Peter, Matt. xxvi. 69, when he was assaulted with a stronger temptation, being not upheld and shored up with a mightier hand, notwithstanding former strength, foully fell. And being fallen, in our raisings up again it is Christ that must do the work, 1. By removing; or, 2. Weakening; or 3. Suspending opposite hindrances; 4. And by advancing the power of his grace in us, to a further degree than we had before we fell; therefore when we are fallen, and by falls have gotten a bruise, let us go to Christ presently to bind us up again.

Use. Let us know, therefore, that it is dangerous to look for that from ourselves which we must have from Christ. Since the fall, all our strength lies in him, as Samson's in his hair, Judges xvi. 17; we are but subordinate agents, moving as we are moved, and working as we are first wrought upon, free so far forth as we are freed, no wiser nor stronger than he makes us to be for the present in anything we undertake. It is his Spirit that actuates and enliveneth, and applieth that knowledge and strength we have, or else it faileth and lieth as useless in us; we work when we work upon a present strength; therefore, dependent spirits are the wisest and the ablest. Nothing is stronger than humility, that goeth out of itself; or weaker than pride, that resteth upon its own bottom, *Frustra nititur qui non innititur;* and this should the rather be observed, because naturally we affect a kind of divinity, *affectatio divinitatis,* in sitting upon actions in the strength of our own parts; whereas Christ saith, "Without me you," apostles that are in a state of grace, "can do nothing," John xv. 5 : he doth not say you can do a little, but nothing. Of ourselves, how easily are we overcome! how weak to resist! we are as reeds shaken with every wind; we shake at the very noise and thought of poverty, disgrace, losses, etc.; we give in presently, we have no power over our eyes, tongues, thoughts, affections, but let sin pass in and out. How soon are we overcome of evil! whereas we should overcome evil with good. How many good purposes stick in the birth, and have no strength to come forth! all which shews how nothing we are without the Spirit of Christ. We see how weak the apostles themselves were, till they were endued with strength from above, Matt. xxvi. 69. Peter was blasted with the speech of a damsel, but after the Spirit of Christ fell upon them, the more they suffered, the more they were encouraged to suffer; their comforts grew with their troubles; therefore in all, especially difficult encounters, let us lift up our hearts to Christ, who hath Spirit enough for us all, in all our exigencies, and say with good Jehoshaphat, "Lord, we know not what to do, but our eyes are towards thee," 2 Chron. xx. 12; the battle we fight is thine, and the strength whereby we fight must be thine. If thou goest not out with us, we are sure to be foiled. Satan knows nothing can prevail against Christ, or those that rely upon his power; therefore his study is, how to keep us in ourselves, and in the creature: but we must carry this always in our minds, that that which is begun in self-confidence will end in shame.

The manner of Christ's *bringing forth judgment to victory*, is by letting us see a necessity of dependence upon him; hence proceed those spiritual desertions wherein he often leaveth us to ourselves, both in regard of grace and comfort, that we may know the spring-head of these to be out of ourselves. Hence it is that in the mount, that is, in extremities, God is most seen, Gen. xxii. 13. Hence it is that we are saved by the grace of faith, that carrieth us out of ourselves to rely upon another; and that faith worketh best alone, when it hath least outward support. Hence it is, that we often fail in lesser conflicts, and stand out in greater, because in lesser we rest more in ourselves, in greater we fly to the rock of our salvation, which is higher than we, Ps. lxi. 2. Hence likewise it is, that we are stronger after foils, because hidden corruption, undiscerned before, is now discovered, and thence we are brought to make use of mercy pardoning, and power supporting. One main ground of this dispensation is, that we should know it is Christ that giveth both the will and the deed, and that as a voluntary work according to his own good pleasure. And therefore we should "work out our salvation in a jealous fear and trembling," Phil. ii. 12, lest by unreverent and presumptuous walking, we give him cause to suspend his gracious influence, and to leave us to the darkness of our own heart.

Those that are under Christ's government have the spirit of revelation, whereby they see and feel a divine power sweetly and strongly enabling them for to preserve faith when they feel the contrary, and hope in a state hopeless, and love to God under signs of his displeasure, and heavenly-mindedness in the midst of worldly affairs and allurements drawing a contrary way. They feel a power preserving patience, nay, joy in the midst of causes of mourning, inward peace in the midst of assaults. Whence is it that, when we are assaulted with temptation, and when compassed with troubles, we have stood out, but from a secret strength upholding us? To make so little grace so victorious over so great a mass of corruption, this requireth a spirit more than human; this is as to preserve fire in the sea, and a part of heaven even as it were in hell. Here we know where to have this power, and to whom to return the praise of it. And it is our happiness, that it is so safely hid in Christ for

us, in one so near unto God and us. Since the
fall, God will not trust us with our own salvation, but it is both purchased and kept by Christ
for us, and we for it through faith, wrought by
the power of God, and laying hold of the same:
which power is gloriously set forth by St. Paul,
1. To be a great power; 2. An exceeding power;
3. A working and a mighty power; 4. Such a
power as was wrought in raising Christ from the
dead, Eph. i. 19. That grace which is but a per-
suasive offer, and in our pleasure to receive or
refuse, is not that grace which brings us to
heaven; but God's people feel a powerful work of
the Spirit, not only revealing unto us our misery,
and deliverance through Christ, but emptying us
of ourselves, as being redeemed from ourselves,
and infusing new life into us, and after strength-
ening us, and quickening of us when we droop
and hang the wing, and never leaving us till
perfect conquest.

CHAP. XXVII.—*Victory not to be had without fighting.*

The sixth conclusion is, that this prevailing
government shall not be without fighting. There
can no be no victory where there is no combat.
In Isaiah it is said, " He shall bring judgment in

truth," Isa. xlii. 3 ; here it is said, he shall send forth judgment unto victory. The word " send forth" hath a stronger sense in the original, to send forth with force ; to shew, that where his government is in truth, it will be opposed, until he getteth the upper hand. Nothing is so opposed as Christ and his government, both within us and without us. And within us most in our conversion, though corruption prevails not so far as to make void the powerful work of grace; yet there is not only a possibility of opposing, but a proneness to oppose ; and not only a proneness, but an actual withstanding the working of Christ's Spirit, and that in every action ; but yet no prevailing resistance so far as to make void the work of grace, but corruption in the issue yields to grace.

There is much ado to bring Christ into the heart, and to set a tribunal for him to judge there; there is an army of lusts in mutiny against him. The utmost strength of most men's endeavours and parts is to keep Christ from ruling in the soul ; the flesh still laboureth to maintain its own regency, and therefore it cries down the credit of whatsoever crosseth it, as God's blessed ordinances, etc., and highly prizeth anything, though never so dead and empty, if it give way to the liberty of the flesh.

And no marvel if the spiritual government of Christ be so opposed: 1. Because it is government, and that limits the course of the will, and casteth a bridle upon its wanderings; everything natural resists what opposeth it; so corrupt will labours to bear down all laws, and counteth it a generous thing not to be awed, and an argument of a low spirit to fear any, even God himself, until unavoidable danger seizeth on men, and then those that feared least out of danger fear most in danger, as we see in Belshazzar, Dan. v. 6.

2. It is spiritual government, and therefore the less will flesh endure it. Christ's government bringeth the very thoughts and desires, which are the most immediate and free issue of the soul, into obedience. Though a man were of so composed a carriage, that his whole life were free from outward offensive breaches, yet with Christ to be "carnally or worldly minded is death," Rom. viii. 6: he looketh on a worldly mind with a greater detestation than any one particular offence.

But Christ's spirit is in those who are in some degree earthly minded.

Truth it is, but not as an allower and maintainer, but as an opposer, subduer, and in the end as a conqueror. Carnal men would fain bring Christ and the flesh together, and could be content with some reservation to submit to Christ; but Christ will be no underling to any base affection; and therefore, where there is allowance of ourselves in any sinful lust, it is a sign the keys were never given up to Christ to rule us.

3. Again, this judgment is opposed, because it is judgment, and men love not to be judged and censured. Now Christ, in his truth, arraigneth them, giveth sentence against them, and bindeth them over to the latter judgment of the great day. And therefore they take upon them to judge that truth that must judge them; but truth will be too good for them. Man hath a day now, which St. Paul calls "man's day," 1 Cor. iv. 33, wherein he getteth upon his bench, and usurpeth a judgment over Christ and his ways; but God hath a day wherein he will set all straight, and his judgment shall stand. And the saints shall have their time, when they shall sit in judgment upon them that judge them now, 1 Cor. vi. 2. In the meantime, Christ will rule in the midst of his enemies, Ps. cx. 3, even in the midst of our hearts.

Use. It is, therefore, no sign of a good condition to find all quiet, and nothing at odds; for can we think that corruption, which is the elder in us, and Satan, the strong man, that keepeth many holds in us, will yield possession quietly? No; there is not so much as a thought of goodness discovered by him, but he joineth with corruption to kill it in the birth. And as Pharaoh's cruelty was especially against the male children, so Satan's malice is especially against the most religious and manly resolutions.

This, then, we are always to expect, that wheresoever Christ cometh, there will be opposition. When Christ was born all Jerusalem was troubled; so when Christ is born in any man, the soul is in an uproar, and all because the heart is unwilling to yield up itself to Christ to rule it.

Wheresoever Christ cometh he breedeth division, not only, 1, between man and himself; but, 2, between man and man; and, 3, between church and church: of which disturbance Christ is no more the cause than physic is of trouble in a distempered body, of which noisome humours are the proper cause; for the end of physic is the peace of humours. But Christ thinketh it fit that the thoughts of men's hearts should be discovered, and he is as well for the falling as the rising of many in Israel, Luke ii. 34.

Thus the desperate madness of men is laid

open, that they had rather be under the guidance of their own lusts, and by consequence of Satan himself, to their endless destruction, than put their feet into Christ's fetters, and their necks under his yoke; whereas, indeed, Christ's service is the only true liberty. His yoke is an easy yoke, his burden but as the burden of wings to a bird, that maketh her fly the higher. Satan's government is rather a bondage than a government, unto which Christ giveth up those that shake off his own, for then he giveth Satan and his factors power over them, since they will not "receive the truth in love," 2 Thess. ii. 20: take him, Jesuit, take him, Satan, blind him and bind him and lead him to perdition. Those that take the most liberty to sin are the most perfect slaves, because most voluntary slaves. The will in everything is either the best or the worst; the further men go on in a wilful course, the deeper they sink in rebellion; and the more they cross Christ, doing what they will, the more they shall one day suffer what they would not. In the meantime, they are prisoners in their own souls, bound over in their consciences to the judgment of him after death, whose judgment they would none of in their lives. And is it not equal that they should feel him a severe judge to condemn them, whom they would not have a mild judge to rule them ?

CHAP. XXVIII.—*Be encouraged to go on cheerfully, with confidence of prevailing.*

For conclusion and general application of all that hath been spoken, unto ourselves. We see the conflicting, but yet sure and hopeful state of God's people. The victory lieth not upon us, but upon Christ, who hath taken upon him, as to conquer for us, so to conquer in us. The victory lieth neither in our own strength to get, nor in our enemies to defeat it. If it lay upon us, we might justly fear. But Christ will maintain his own government in us, and take our part against our corruptions ; they are his enemies as well as ours. " Let us therefore be strong in the Lord, and in the power of his might," Eph. vi. 10; let us not look so much who are our enemies, as who is our judge and captain, nor what they threaten, but what he promiseth. We have more for us than against us. What coward would not fight when he is sure of victory ? None are here overcome, but he that will not fight. Therefore, when any base fainting seizeth upon us, let us lay the blame where it is to be laid.

Discouragement rising from unbelief and ill report, brought upon the good land by the spies, moved God to swear in his wrath, that they should not enter into his rest. Let us take heed a spirit of faint-heartedness, rising from seeming difficulty and disgrace, cast upon God's good ways, provoke not God to keep us out of heaven. We see here what we may look for from heaven. O beloved, it is a comfortable thing to conceive of Christ aright, to know what love, mercy, strength, we have laid up for us in the breast of Christ. A good conceit of the physician, we say, is half the cure ; let us make use of this his mercy and power every day, in our daily combats. Lord Jesus, thou hast promised not to quench the smoking flax, not to break the bruised reed ; cherish thine own grace in me, leave me not to myself, the glory shall be thine. Let us not suffer Satan to transform Christ unto us, to be otherwise than he is to those that are his. Christ will not leave us, till he hath made us like himself, "all glorious within and without, and presenteth us blameless before his Father," Jude 24. What a comfort is this in our conflicts with our unruly hearts, that it shall not always be thus! Let us strive a little while, and we shall be happy for ever. Let us think when we are troubled with our sins, that Christ hath this in charge of his Father, "that he shall not quench the smoking flax," until he hath subdued all. This putteth a shield into our hands to beat back all "the fiery darts of Satan," Eph. vi. 16. He will object, (1.) thou art a great sinner; we may answer, Christ is a strong Saviour; but he will object, (2.) thou hast no faith, no love; yes, a spark of faith and love; but (3.) Christ will not regard that; yes, "he will not quench the smoking flax;" but (4.) this is so little and weak, that it will vanish and come to nought: nay, but Christ will cherish it, until he hath brought judgment to victory. And thus much for our comfort we have already, that even when we first believed, we overcame God himself, as it were, by believing the pardon of all our sins; notwithstanding the guilt of our own consciences, and his absolute justice. Now, having been prevailers with God, what shall stand against us if we can learn to make use of our faith?

Oh, what a confusion is this to Satan, that he should labour to blow out a poor spark, and yet should not be able to quench it; that a grain of mustard seed should be stronger than the gates of hell; that it should be able to remove mountains of oppositions and temptations cast up by

Satan and our rebellious hearts between God and us. Abimelech could not endure that it should be said "a woman had slain him," Judges ix. 54; and it must needs be a torment to Satan, that a weak child, a woman, and decrepit old man should, by a spirit of faith, put him to flight.

Since there is such comfort where there is a little truth of grace, that it will be so victorious, let us oft try what God hath wrought in us, search our good as well as our ill, and be thankful to God for the least measure of grace, more than for any outward thing; it will be of more use and comfort than all this world, which passeth away and cometh to nothing. Yea, let us be thankful for that promised and assured victory, which we may rely on without presumption, as St. Paul doth; "thanks be to God, that hath given us victory in Jesus Christ," 1 Cor. xv. 57. See a flame in a spark, a tree in a seed; see great things in little beginnings; look not so much to the beginning, as to the perfection, and so we shall be in some degree joyful in ourselves, and thankful unto Christ.

Neither must we reason from a denial of a great measure of grace, to a denial of any at all in us; for faith and grace stand not in an indivisible point, so as he that hath not such and such a measure hath none at all; but as there is a great breadth between a spark and a flame, so there is a great wideness between the least measure of grace and the greatest; and he that hath the least measure, is within the compass of God's eternal favour; though he be not a shining light, yet he is a smoking wick, which Christ's tender care will not suffer him to quench.

And let all this that hath been spoken allure those that are not yet in state of grace, to come under Christ's sweet and victorious government, for though we shall have much opposition, yet if we strive, he will help us; if we fail, he will cherish us; if we be guided by him, we shall overcome; if we overcome, we are sure to be crowned. And for the present state of the church, we see now how forlorn it is, yet let us comfort ourselves, that Christ's cause shall prevail; "Christ will rule, till he hath made his enemies his footstool," Ps. cx. 1, not only to trample upon, but to help him up to mount higher in glory. "Babylon shall fall, for strong is the Lord who hath condemned her," Rev. xviii. 8. Christ's judgment not only in his children, but also against his enemies, shall be victorious, for he is " King of kings and Lord of lords," Rev. xix. 1.   God will not always suffer antichrist and his supports to revel and ruffle in the church as they do.

If we look to the present state of the church of Christ, it is as Daniel in the midst of lions, as a lily amongst thorns, as a ship not only tossed, but almost covered with waves. It is so low, that the enemies think they have buried Christ, in regard of his gospel, in the grave, and there they think to keep him from rising; but Christ as he rose in his person, so he will roll away all stones, and rise again in his church.   How little support hath the church and cause of Christ at this day! how strong a conspiracy is against it! the spirit of antichrist is now lifted up, and marcheth furiously; things seem to hang on a small and invisible thread.   But our comfort is, that Christ liveth and reigneth and standeth on Mount Sion in defence of them that stand for him, Rev. xiv. 1 ; and when states and kindgoms shall dash one against another, Christ will have care of his own children and cause, seeing there is nothing else in the world that he much esteemeth.   At this very time the delivery of his church, and the ruin of his enemies, is in working ; we see no things in motion till Christ hath done his work, and then we shall see that the Lord reigneth.

Christ and his church, when they are at the lowest, are nearest rising: his enemies at the highest are nearest a downfall.

The Jews are not yet come in under Christ's banner; but God, that hath persuaded Japhet to come into the tents of Shem, will persuade Shem to come into the tents of Japhet, Gen. ix. 27. The "fulness of the Gentiles is not yet come in," Rom. xi. 25, but Christ, that hath the "utmost parts of the earth given him for his possession," Ps. ii. 8, will gather all the sheep his Father hath given him into one fold, that there may be one sheepfold, and one Shepherd, John x. 16.

The faithful Jews rejoiced to think of the calling of the Gentiles; and why should not we joy to think of the calling of the Jews?

The gospel's course hath hitherto been as that of the sun, from east to west, and so in God's time may proceed yet further west. No creature can hinder the course of the sun, nor stop the influence of heaven, nor hinder the blowing of the wind, much less hinder the prevailing power of divine truth, until Christ hath brought all under one head, and then he will present all to his Father; these are they thou hast given unto me; these are they that have taken me for their Lord and King, that have suffered with me; my will is that they be where I am, and reign with me. And then he will deliver up the kingdom even to his Father, and put down all other rule, and authority, and power, 1 Cor. xv. 24.

Let us then bring our hearts to holy resolutions, and set ourselves upon that which is good, and against that which is ill, in ourselves or others, according to our callings, upon this encouragement, that Christ's grace and power shall go along with us. What had become of that great work of reformation of religion in the latter-spring of the gospel, if men had not been armed with invincible courage to outstride all lets, upon this faith, that the cause was Christ's, and that he would not be wanting to his own cause. Luther ingenuously confessed, that he carried matters often inconsiderately, and with mixture of passion; but upon acknowledgment, God took not advantage of his errors, but the cause being God's, and his aims being holy, to promote the truth, and being a mighty man in prayer, and strong in faith, God by him kindled that fire which all the world shall never be able to quench. According to our faith, so is our encouragement to all duties, therefore let us strengthen faith, that it may strengthen all other graces. This very belief, that faith shall be victorious, is a means to make it so indeed. Believe it, therefore, that though it be often as smoking flax, yet it shall prevail. If it prevail with God himself in trials, shall it not prevail over all other opposition? "Let us wait awhile, and we shall see the salvation of the Lord," Exod. iv. 13.

The Lord reveal himself more and more unto us in the face of his Son Jesus Christ, and magnify the power of his grace in cherishing those beginnings of grace in the midst of our corruptions, and sanctify the consideration of our own infirmities to humble us, and of his tender mercy to encourage us; and persuade us, that since he hath taken us into the covenant of grace, he will not cast us off for those corruptions; which as they grieve his Spirit, so they make us vile in our own eyes. And because Satan labours to obscure the glory of his mercy, and hinder our comfort by discouragements, the Lord add this to the rest of his mercies, that, since he is so gracious to those that yield to his government, we may make the right use of this grace, and not lose any portion of comfort that is laid up for us in Christ. And may he vouchsafe to let the prevailing power of his Spirit in us be an evidence of the truth of grace begun, and a pledge of final victory, at that time when he will be all in all, in all his, for all eternity. AMEN.

Printed by FRANK MURRAY, *11 Young Street, Edinburgh.*